# DISCOVERY

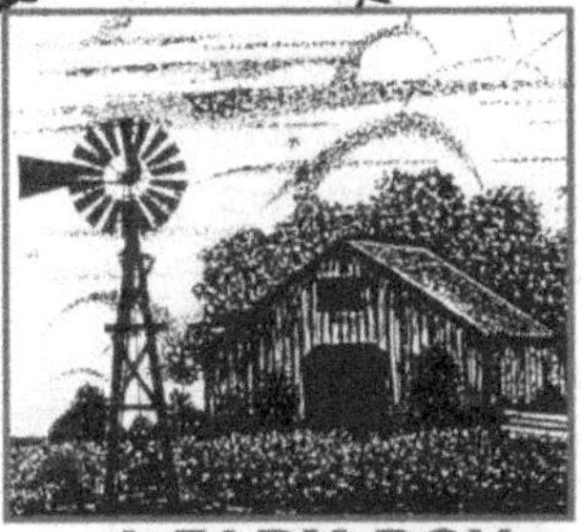

A FARM BOY

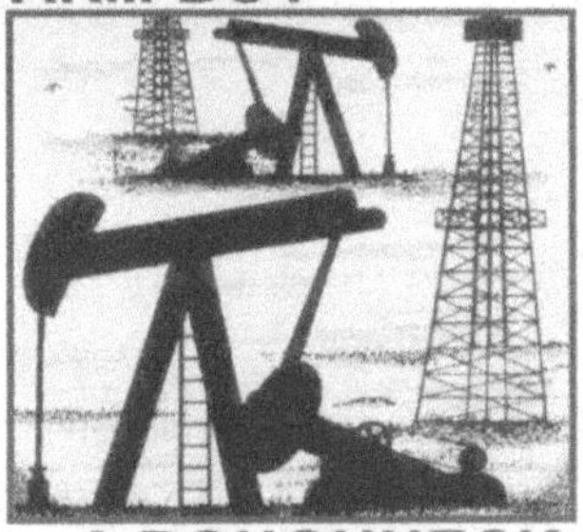

A ROUGHNECK

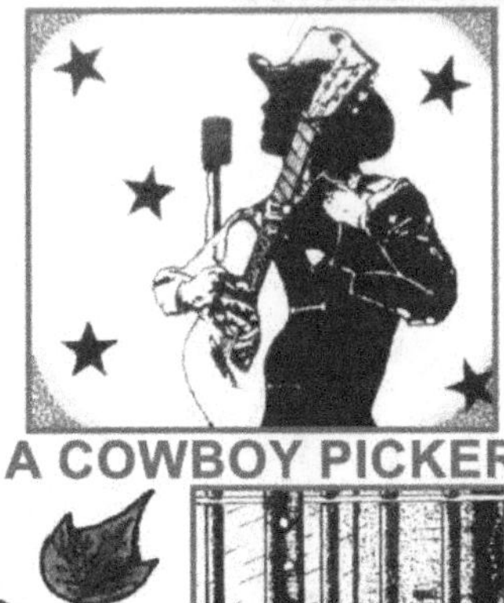

A COWBOY PICKER

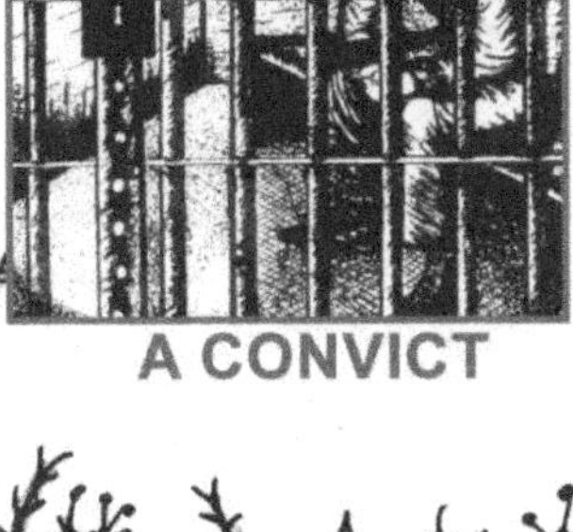

A CONVICT

## Poetry and Art
## by
## Rick and Jan Sikes

DISCOVERY



Cover Design, Interior Design and Typesetting
by Donna Osborn Clark at: www.creationbydonna.com

All art inside book created by Rick Sikes
Websites: www.ricksikes.com
www.jansikes.com

ISBN 978-0-9906179-6-9

Published by:
RIJAN PUBLISHING
www.rijanpublishing.com

Manufactured in the United States of America

First Edition

## *Foreword*

In 1976, while I was married to country singer-songwriter, Willie Nelson, I tried to answer as much of Willie's fan mail as I could. I intercepted a letter to Willie, which started a friendship for me that changed my life.

That letter was from a prisoner in Leavenworth Penitentiary. He sent, with his letter, some incredible artwork (to the best of my memory, it was a beautifully hand-tooled leather wallet for Willie). Over the next few years, he would send more of his art, exceptional poetry and songs. But, as spectacular as his artistic talent was, the 'heart' of his letters were what changed my life.

His genuine love for Willie was more than apparent, but what inspired me and drew me to build a friendship, was his love of beauty and his never ending, unbroken spirit. He never bought into discouragement or despair - he exuded only beauty. Willie used to always say these words, "Let only good come to you and let only good come from you!" No one I knew exemplified that better than Rick Sikes.

I am so honored to get to know Jan, who gave him unconditional love and is passing his legacy of beauty on for us all to enjoy, and for her giving me this chance to show how much Rick's friendship and art meant to me and made my life better.

Connie Nelson

## *The Artwork*

Millions of tiny dots create the unique art by Rick Sikes, displayed in this book. It has a name, Pointillism, but I prefer to think of it as Rick's unique style of creating.

He used simple pen-and-ink to create what you will find here. Some pieces took him hundreds of hours to complete. But, as he often said, he had nothing but time on his hands while existing behind the walls of prison.

He is an inspiration to anyone facing hard times, depression and or oppression. He never gave up. He looked for ways to express positive thought and action throughout the long years of incarceration.

Not only did he create pen-and-ink drawings like these, but he tooled leather, painted with oils, did Native American bead work, fired one-of-a-kind ceramic pieces and produced hundreds of songs and poems.

Let this book be your ray of hope, your encouragement when the going gets tough and your motivation to reach higher.

I invite you to examine each piece of Rick's art where you'll discover a bit of the soul from the man who created them.

*Table of Contents*

# RICK - BREATHS OF LIFE FROM A PRISON CELL

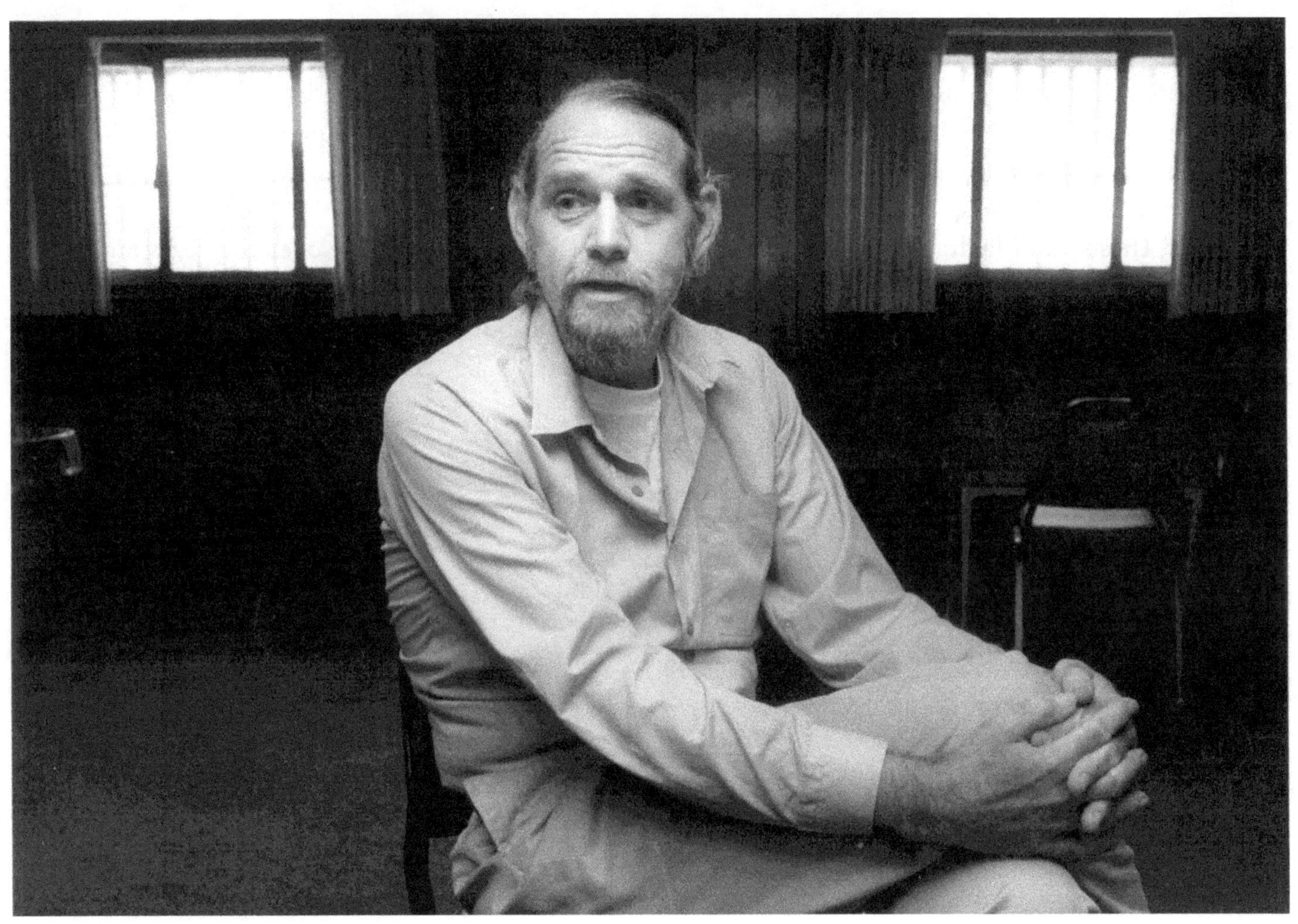

# *Letter From Rick*

From December 12, 1971 until August 16, 1985, I had the misfortune of being a "resident" at the U.S. Penitentiary in Leavenworth, Kansas; although not a voluntary visit. Being on the inside looking out and not burdened by the daily normal concerns in outside living, one has much time for soul-searching, reminiscing and realizing basic needs that are unfilled due to denial of freedom.

I learned much about myself and other beings. In this fourteen year (plus) journey, I put to pen many of my deepest thoughts, soul yearnings and observations. I wrote songs, painted, did bead work, pottery, and leather craft, received my G.E.D., as well as doing my prison job assignment. I found time to correspond with over 100 people on the outside.

Finally, these humble drawings and writings in this little book were done over the years and reflect the sincere feelings going through my mind at the time that they were done. Some in times of severe loneliness, despair, and some in an "off-the-wall" sense of humor I possess, which helped me fight off depression.

In truth, these were 'Etched in Stone' day by day, bit by bit on this pilgrimage of self DISCOVERY.

Rick Sikes
#87047-132

## *Discovery*

Through life's wilderness I wandered aimlessly seeking my way
Seldom looking up to see the light of day
Stumbling blindly, 'til so weary, I could go no more
In total exhaustion I fell to the earthen floor
My eyes focused upon a wounded but lovely thing
Seemingly an angel felled with a broken wing
Said I, "Stranger, what will be your name?"
A voice spoke softly, "Yours, for our names are the same."
I replied angrily, "That cannot be."
In understanding the voice spoke again, "Look and you shall see."
"What song do you sing?" I asked, as I drew nearer
"Your song my friend, listen and you shall hear."
"You know me?" said I, as the sweet melody began to flow.
"From the very first," the voice whispered. " Yes, you I know."
"You are fantasy, you are imagination, and you're not real."
Patiently the voice said in a soft tone, "Satisfy your doubt, touch and feel."
I shouted, "You are the Death-Angel that has come to take me away."
"No, I am faith and compassion left behind yesterday."
I replied, "When others are worthy, why did a wretch like me, you select?"
The gentle voice asked, "Who is the being my eyes reflect?"
In the kind loving eyes sparkled, an image of me,
Not the hopeless, cast-out soul, I thought myself to be.
The spirit smiled and said, "I saw your need and I came."
Respectfully, I asked, "How can you help me, when you yourself are lame?"
"Truth, but my wound does not exceed your own,
My friend, together we shall mend and then travel on,
Walking slowly and cautiously, gradually regaining our strength.
In confidence and with patience, our stride will soon reach full length.
For in peace, love and understanding you shall stay,
In your heart, I will dwell, no matter how hard the way."
Leaving behind the dark wilderness, where lost I had been,
To tread upon a sure path, that is lit from within.

# THE WORLD CAN BE YOURS

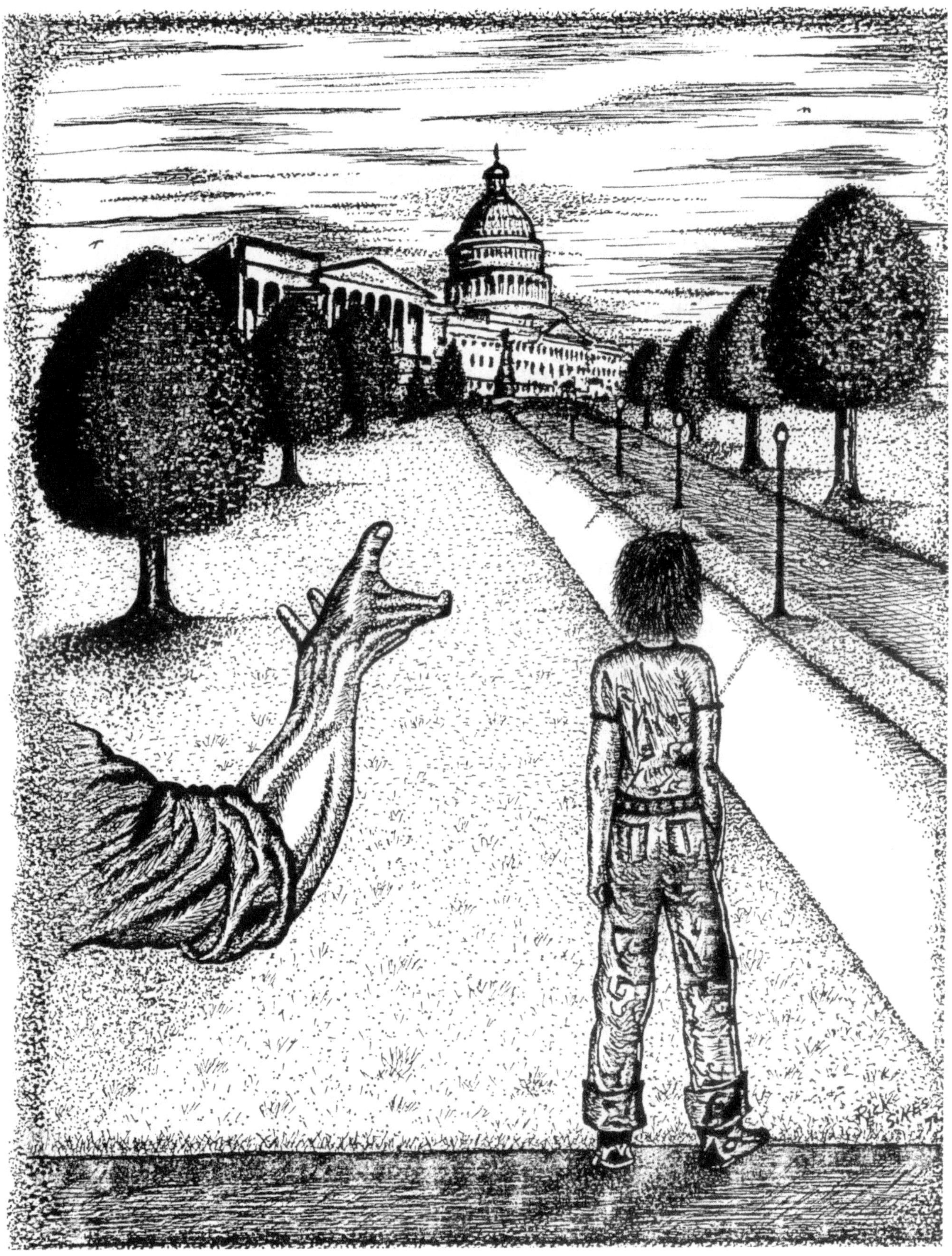

## *Free Children's Song*

Sing little children, sing for me

Though we are many miles apart

Long have I been in chains, but now I am free

A freed spirit song lives within my heart

Sing a happy song for the world to hear

Sing your song gaily, don't ever cry

You are the heart of the land we hold dear

Sing in faith, I'll be home by and by

Let your laughter ring with sliver bell tone

Be you not frightened by the howling wind

Look up, the light shines, you are not alone,

Nature brings to you, gifts of love I send

Your songs shall conquer, tyrants must fail

Smile; remember me in your prayer

Before your song has ended, I'll be there.

## *Master of My Way*

A spin of the wheel, turn of the card
Can change one's destiny
Ask a bum in any railroad yard
To be sure that you plainly see
They tell of how things went wrong
And lament their sorrowful hymn
Sing their poor ole' hobo's song
Of how fate is against them
Begging for pity and a handout
Sadness, tears are cried
Hungry, ragged, no doubt
Fail to admit, they never tried
Don't blame it on astrology
Crystal balls or fortune cookies
There is no need for apology
For odds bring marks to bookies
Losers bet on the chances
Winners cater to cinches
Creating their own circumstances
All are proven in the clinches
If my life turns bad today
I'll not wait on bad times to pass
For I am the master of my way
It's all luck – my ass
Trouble has no friends
Winners win from losers
Distillers make the blends
Pushers have their users
Preachers, ramblers, ladies of the night
Players in people games and stakes are high
Forever arguing wrong and right
But, never understanding why

## *Common Folks*

So many common folks doing without

Wrapped up in their own things, no doubt

From love nights, to labor in the morning new

Finding courage to see each day through

Working and believing, come what may

Living, loving, waiting for a better day

If it was good enough for those gone before

Why then ask for better or any more

Hands full of nothing, hearts full of dreams

Living on hope today, for whatever tomorrow brings

## *Deeds and Rewards of Men and Bards*

Toward seas the rivers invariably run

Souls are marked eternally by deeds done

Those of honor fully live each day

Lesser beings must hold the past at bay

True people need not bow in shame

Cowards must always bear their blame

Oak trees do not bend so far

As to break and scar

Mighty mountains do not tumble

Nor do they quake and crumble

From their outer sides no doubt

Destruction is from within, not without

Rivers shall forever flow

The strong oak ever grow

Though seas may angrily lash

Majestic mountains may crash

Honorable people will stand proud and tall

The weak ones shall always fall

## *The Rich, The Poor*

The rich grow richer
The poor grow poorer
While the Wee-folk dance in the wilderness
The rich and poor suffer
In their different unhappiness
Tis indeed a pity to be
Too rich or too poor
To miss the lively songs
The dancing in the moor
When the grawls quieten
For the kailee
Think, to give of thyself
Is but to reward thee
The Gean Canach may take your wife
The Leanhaun Shee might take your life
But, sadder sure
The ungrateful rich
The lazy poor
For they shall miss
The ceo'l-sidhe of the moor

## *A Preacher, A Chicken, A Sunday*

Yesterday, I was a boy on the farm

How those years have flown

I think of youth, folks back home

All the good times we have known

Sunday morning we could hear

The old church bell tolling clear

Through the hills so sweetly ringing

Preaching and lots of happy singing

Kinfolks visiting, chicken frying

Kids playing, old folks praying

Sundays were fun days

I never listened much to

What the preacher said

Though oft times a few of those things

Will run through my head

But, being a rebel I chose my way

Still in my cell, I dream of going home someday

To a preacher, a chicken, and a Sunday

# *ALONE WITH PEN AND PAPER*

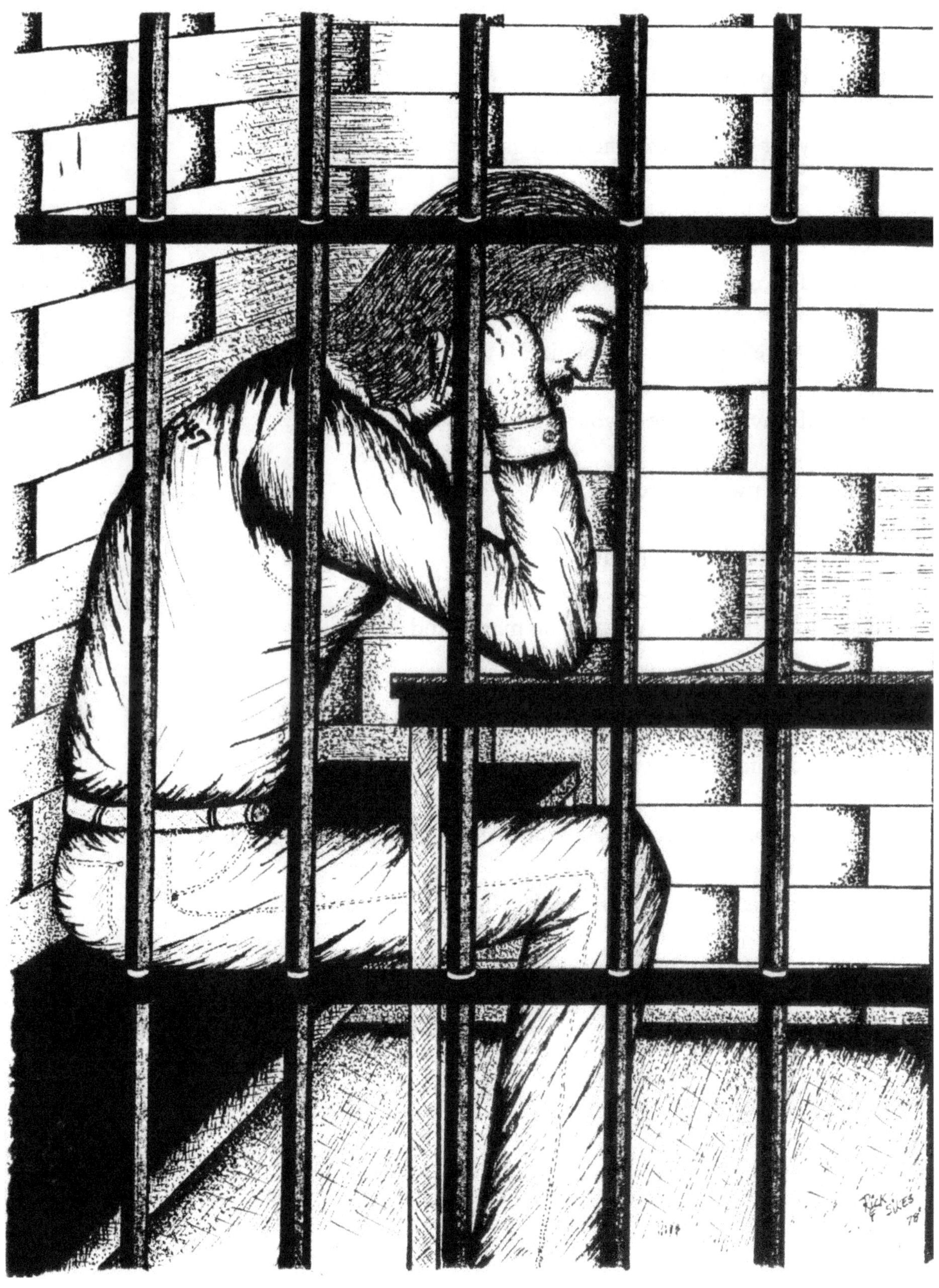

## *Paper Man*

I sit alone with pen in hand

Visualizing your many needs and feelings

Knowing it must be lonely loving a paper man

No one could love you as much as I

As you read these lines please recognize

My very soul craves and needs you

I realize that your world is reality

Mine is exiled existence in duality

Secluded with self sought fantasy in no man's land

You in my arms is my dream, my plan

With love and emotion, on paper I send my heart

Sincere expressions of devotion across the miles I impart

Time will bring us together, with the shifting of the sand

Have faith, look up, and continue loving your paper man

## *Prisoner To Press*

You say you are a writer
And want to know how prisoners feel
I can't tell you now
And no one ever will
Words don't describe being forsaken
Lost and alone
It's just feeling until
All the feeling is gone
While life is wasting forever
As time drags slowly by
Seems that no one cares
But, you keep wondering why
Thinking of walking out "that" door
'Til hope dies, to live no more
You believe until the last dreams shatter
Afterward, it just doesn't matter
Hanging on when there's nothing
Left to hang on to
'Til all that's hanging...is you
I have confused you, no doubt
Said nothing that you can write about
I told you straight and face to face
But, the only way to really know
Is to be in a prisoner's place

## *Sexual Revolution*

Yesterday is over and worn
The new day being born

New people, all races

See the now look on faces

Changing trends, changing styles

Happy moods and smiles

There is reason why

Don't let it pass you by

A man and a woman

Or your soul solution

Everyone loving and living

It's sexual revolution

Contented folks are getting

You can be betting

They aren't puppets on a string

But people doing their thing

It's time for trying

Moments are swiftly flying

You must understand

The time is at hand

Accept what nature's giving

Really get into living

Get it together

Nothing lasts forever

## *Love Comes Love Goes*

I don't know where girls are gringo

I know where love

Lived one time though

In a small room above the cabaret

But nothing will forever stay

Even down in Mexico

Senorita held his hand amigo

She loved that man and it did show

"Si," she told him so

She wanted to be his alone

Crying long after he was gone

She begged him, "Please don't go"

He was a fool that guy

Leaving her to cry

In time the bad winds blow

Then she moved far away

From the room above the cabaret

I suppose love comes…love goes

# *Standing In Line*

As a kid I remember standing in line for shoes outgrown
Guess I'll be standing in line from now on
Standing in line for my clothes, in line for my chow
I've spent my life standing in line somehow
Stand in line for a job to work my life away
Then stand in line for my pay
I once had a woman, I thought was true
I found I was standing in line for her too
Spending my life reaching for a star
Standing in line to sing and play my guitar
Waiting for a dream to come through
Standing in line is all I do
This ole' in-line life
Fills my soul with grief and strife
Stand in line 'til I'm bent and old
Standing in line for parole
Boss said, "Walk slow, stand in line
We'll let you know when you've done your time"
So, I'll stand until they let me know
Standing in line watching my life come and go

## *Beautiful Roses, Cotton-Candy, Peppermint, and Popcorn Prison Blues*

If they throw a poor boy in jail
Hold him without any bail
Feed him beans and bread that's stale
If the blind-frigid bitch justice should fail
Railroaded right on down the rail
Down the river without a sail
Throw his mangy carcass in a cell
Cuss him, kick his ol' tail
Starve him 'til he's weak and pale
Scream and bitch at him, mess with his mail
Bunk him with whatever weird-o's that may prevail
Blacks using Magic-Shave, what a smell
They say he is finally rehabilitated, all is well
He can go straight now, get a union job, draw scale
Dip honey for a cesspool cleaner, toss hay for farmer in the dell
Work an off-shore rig in Louisiana, drill an oil well
Be a cowboy out in Texas where the coyotes wail
A clerk in a New York Jew store, learn to sell
All kinds of fiction, what phony tales
Mr. X-Con, hits the street lower than whales
After ten years, if he is better off, I can't tell
But, he finds time to write off twenty-three lines of this crap, so what the hell!

# *Trial, Truth, and Trend*

Notable Americans, ladies and gentlemen of the jury, I now charge

There is much at stake, your responsibility is large.

We must be fair and equal in this trial. I'm sure that you realize,

Overwhelming is the evidence before your eyes.

One, a gentleman, an important pillar of our community

Who, actually should have been granted immunity.

This other "person?" whatever, is clearly a social disgrace

Dressed in rags, that long hair and bearded face.

This citizen has afforded his own attorneys from out of town.

This court generously appointed the indigent, the best patent lawyer around.

Perhaps the gentleman was indirectly involved to a minor extent.

It's obvious this vagabond is not even a resident.

The gentleman may be guilty of a slight, harmless infraction, I debate

But, he isn't a rebel filled with violence, malice, nor hate.

We, the people must press for justice, democracy and right!

This belligerent vagrant refused to go to Vietnam to fight.

Could we punish an outstanding man for petty wrongs?

Shouldn't we be more concerned to put this "creature" where he belongs?

Yes, indeed his capable attorney put up a brilliant defense

But, now, in light of this very plain evidence,

I feel you, the jury, being wise, sound and stationary,

Will deal justly with this bearded revolutionary.

The eagle is our national bird; defiantly he wears the symbol of a dove.

Clad in beads and sandals, speaks in public of peace and love.

With all of his passive talk, facts of the law remain still,

This ungrateful delinquent refused to fight, our enemy kill.

True, he is white, but like all of these undesirables who plague our towns,

Those red-men, the blacks, yellows and browns.

Let now my unbiased opinions influence nor blind justice's eye.

Proof stands before you, a useless character, a gentleman in coat and tie.

Obviously, this gentleman's failure to disclose was only oversight.

His accountants and attorneys assure to promptly set it right.

You must decide the gravity and degree of sin,

Pass judgment - give your honest verdict then.

This choice was made two thousand years before.

Now it is your duty, to make it once more.

What your verdict shall be, only you, the jury knows.

In closing, I will say, already the jailers gamble for the Hippie's clothes.

Surely you will release Mr. Barrabas, that remarkable citizen there,

And justly prosecute this bearded one with the long hair.

## *Men Like Me*

The hours and flowers
Are not often gone
Until the seasons of youth
Have so swiftly flown
Battles raged throughout the years
Against fate's ill decree
Seared, torn, and weary-worn
I wonder if this world
Has a place, for men like me
People coldly shun
Turn without care
Deaf to cries of suffering
Seeking fantasy to hear
Life, played in varied parts
By gentle and fierce hearts
Doles out its casted roles
Even to the realist-misfit souls
Eyes of the people are not blind
They just refuse to see
Denying we even exist
The realist, the fools
Men like me

# *WILLIE*

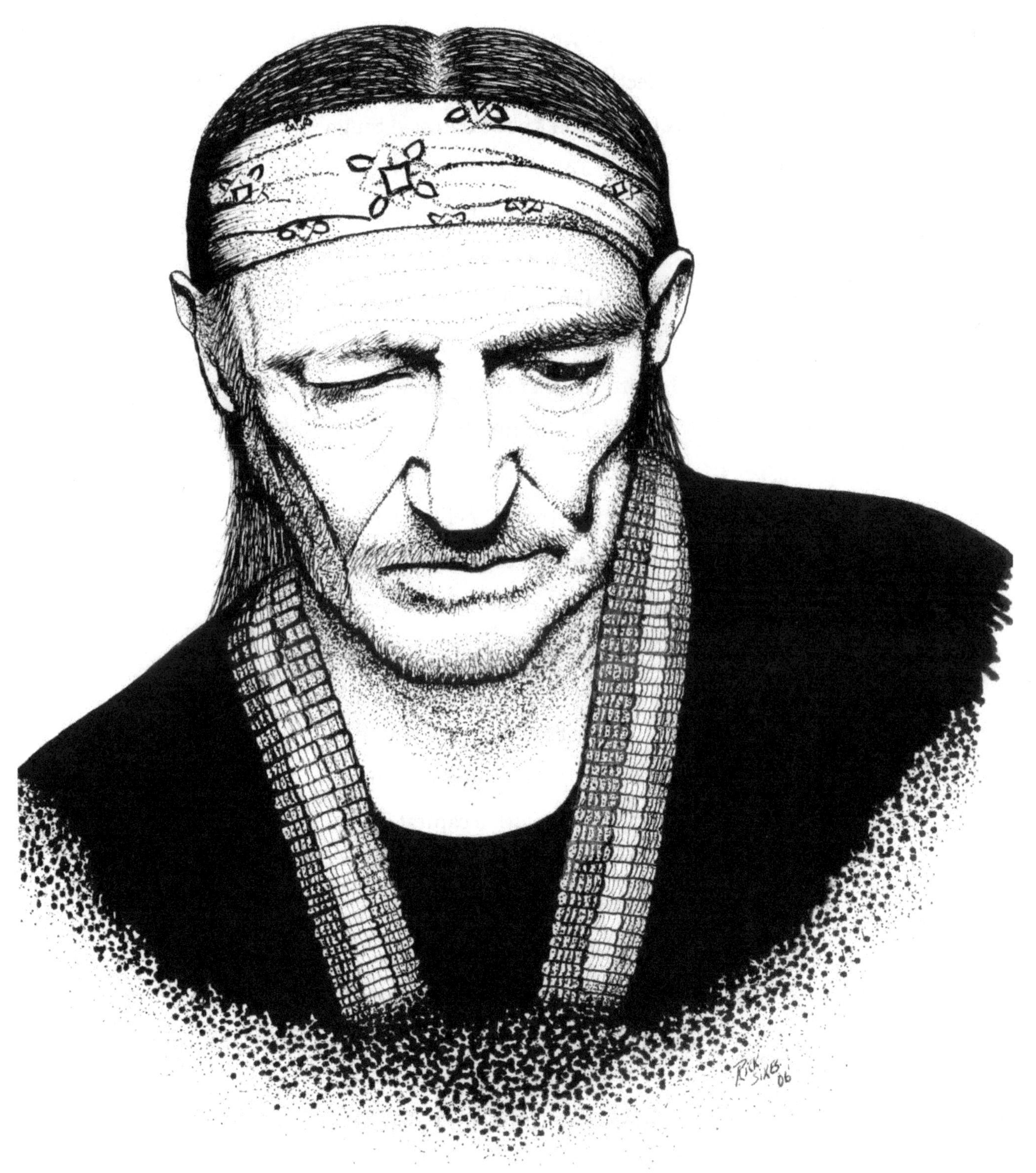

## *Ol' Willie for President*

Folks won't be outta snuff
We 'lect the right guy to runnin' stuff
'N times won't be so damned tough
Now if we vote ol' Willie for the Pressy-dent
We won't get skint
I ain't no sap
An' I'm tired of this crap
That's my senty-ment
I'd shore 'druther see Willie's movies
Than Ronnie Reagan's
'N he grins as good as Jimmy Carter
'Tween th' three, I believe he's a
Helluva lot smarter
Paul for Vice President would be nice
'N 'ol Paul does know 'bout vice
We'd be somebody
Jist bein' ourself
Groceries piled high on th' shelf
Freedom with a capital F
'Ol Willie being Pressy-dent
Little money to be spent
Pay back th' loan
Have a buck of our own
Not owe nobody
Nary a cent
If'n we had ol' Willie for Pressy-dent

## *Ride Down and Raid the Ranch*

Boys it's wrong, just ain't right!

Good as she looked Saturday night.

She was the belle of the ball.

I couldn't help but fall.

You oughta' seen her dance.

Think I'll ride on down and raid the ranch.

The prettiest chick I ever seen,

With that dude, big, bad and mean.

Ain't no doubt, he'll tear me apart.

But she went and won my heart,

With a secret little come-on glance.

Think I'll ride on down and raid the ranch.

A picture of beauty standing there,

Big blue eyes, long dark hair.

That man daring anyone to try,

With clenched fists and eagle eye.

Courage builds with romance.

Think I'll ride on down and raid the ranch.

# *No More 'N Four*

I learned pickin' all by myself.
Didn't need none of that book learnin'.
I got my own style, you might say.
Just natural talent that goes a long way.
What they call commercial songs
Ain't got but a chord or two.
So, I says to me, I'm goin' to Tennessee,
Show them cotton-pickers how.
Down at that Grand Ole' Opry
I'll knock em' right out of the tree!
Some of my songs got three,
Chords, that is,
But, never no more than four.
I hitched me a ride to Nashville.
Boy, was they surprised,
Just like I thought they'd be.
Should of seen the admirin' way
Them folks looked at me.
I'd pop in their offices
And whoop off a tune.
They'd start getting excited
Yellin', "What th' hell's goin' on?"
I'd say, "Jist hold it, I ain't even
Let ya'll hear my singin' yet.
Now, I'm gonna' pick ya'll this here
Nother' little tune.
It's got four, chords, that is,
It'll put you on the floor!"
More'n four is jist' too much for em'.

Later on in th' day, dudes in white suits
Started comin' my way, with a funny lookin' jacket.
Talk about a dream come true
I'll tell you when I heard Ol' Chet
Say, "Take it away", it made my day!
I just knew he would, I'm plenty good.
But them dudes in white grabbed me,
Guitar n' all, throwed me against the wall,
Then pinned me on th' floor.
While they was tyin' me up
I heard Chet saying "That ain't enough,
Tie him with more; tie him with Four, cords, that is."
I mighta' knowed, I blew their minds.
Went way over their heads.
Yeah, way on over.
I really meant no harm.
Some of these cool dudes
Here at this 'funny-farm'
Said I played them Nashville cats
Too damned hard, much too hard.
Plum' caught 'em off guard.
These dudes say the world
Jist ain't ready fer me yet.
Now, I can understand about ol' Chet.
A feller hates to lose his job,
An I shore scared th' hell outta him!
Him and all the rest of them.
I used too many chords.
Like I said before, once in a while
As many as three, on special occasions
Maybe four, no more 'n four, NEVER more 'n four!

## *Do-Little Dandy, Sho' 'Nuff Handyman*

Some folks don't like me
Their reason is easy to see
Cause whey they're gone
Their women get on the phone
Call-up this here dandy
Sweet as candy, sho' nuff' handyman
I'll do it here, do it there
On the sea, on the land
The best of loving
Super heavy turtle-doving
I'm fine and randy
Jim-Dandy, always ready man
Filling the need
My work is guaranteed
Champ at heart, master of the art
Laying them in the shade
I'm the best in the trade
Good as wild honey, most for the money
Number one to get the job done
The ladies depend on me
Feel free to call me anytime
Cause I'll do 'em all right
If it takes all night
Or I'll just hold their hand
I'm sure the best to fill all requests

Some folks can, some folks can't

I never had a complaint

I ain't no saint, but a mighty handy man

I work by day, work by night

I satisfy any appetite

Till all their tensions are eased

Never done it wrong

I ring their bell, bong their gong

They are squeezed, teased and pleased

Service with a smile

That's my style

So remember all the while

Give me a ring, for the real thing

**TELEPHONE RINGS:**

"Hello, yes Ma'am this is the do-little dandy, sho' nuff' handyman. Yes, oh yes, that is one of my specialties; oh hell yeah! I like that too. I think I can fit you into my schedule next week. Yes, yes, Ummmmm! I'm sure looking forward to that. Yes, for sure, yes Ma'am, uh-huh, right-on. I can hardly wait. Pardon, Ma'am, huh? What's that you say? Huh? Your husband too! Hey, you gotta be joking. Hey, what are you, a freak of some kind? You done got yourself a wrong number, I-I-I dunno' what to say. Oh hell no! No way, you get nerve, I'll never...."

## *The Title Is Too Damned Long or (When Aunt Bessie Rode A Bike To The Belly-dancer's Ball)*

Here is a story of a gal with gall
It happened a year ago this fall
When Aunt Bessie rode a bike
To the belly-dancers ball
Aunt Bessie is past sixty-nine
Full of spark, feeling fine
She walked from the farm
A ten mile hike in pouring rain
Just in time to miss the train
She was mad as hell and soaking wet
But swore by heaven, she'd get there yet
She said, "It's better late, than not at all
I'll get there, if I have to crawl
This is gonna be a helluva dance
I ain't gonna' miss my chance."
It's no place for a red-neck square
Roarin'Twenties hoochy-gals gathering there
Aunt Bessie was hitching just out of L.A.
Flipper skirt flapping, she thumbed on the freeway
Fifty bikers pulled up and asked, "You goin' our way?"
Auntie Bessie said, "You got it. This must be my day"
She hopped right on the buddy-seat
She caught a nose full of biker aroma
That was super charged with heat

She said, "Make like this is a race."
Then she pushed his stringy hairs from her face
She read the back of his tee-shirt
Between the dirt, it said, 'spaced-out or outta-space'
He reached beneath her leg into the saddle bag
Fishing out a cold brew
Says, "Babe, I ain't comin' on at you,
But for your age, you're really alive."
She said, "Cool the shit, man, pass the suds,
Hit the gas and cut all the jive."
They pulled in front on the mall
Just as things began to swing
The girls ran giggling saying, "Oh Bessie!
Where did ya' find all the cute boys to bring?"
Everyone started bumping, doing their thing
Letting down their hair, having a fling
Wiggling, squirming, cha-cha-cha
Charleston, black-bottom, ooh-la-la
The greatest ball we've ever had before
More fun than the one in twenty-four
The best by far, no doubt at all
When Aunt Bessie rode a bike to the belly-dancer's ball

## *The Bull in the China Closet*

In fond remembrance
Of the good ol' days
Before women's rights
Put out our lights
When the bull in the
China closet came charging in
Liquored-up for loving on
That ninety-proof gin
Horny as hell, mean as sin
The little woman
Let him have his way
Knowing he'd be sick
And sorry the next day
She had her ways to make him pay
Things aren't the same
Not anymore
The little kitten has begun to roar
She's no meek little mouse
Since lib came to our house
Things sure got quiet around here
Now, the ol' bull feels like a steer

# *DREAM VISITS*

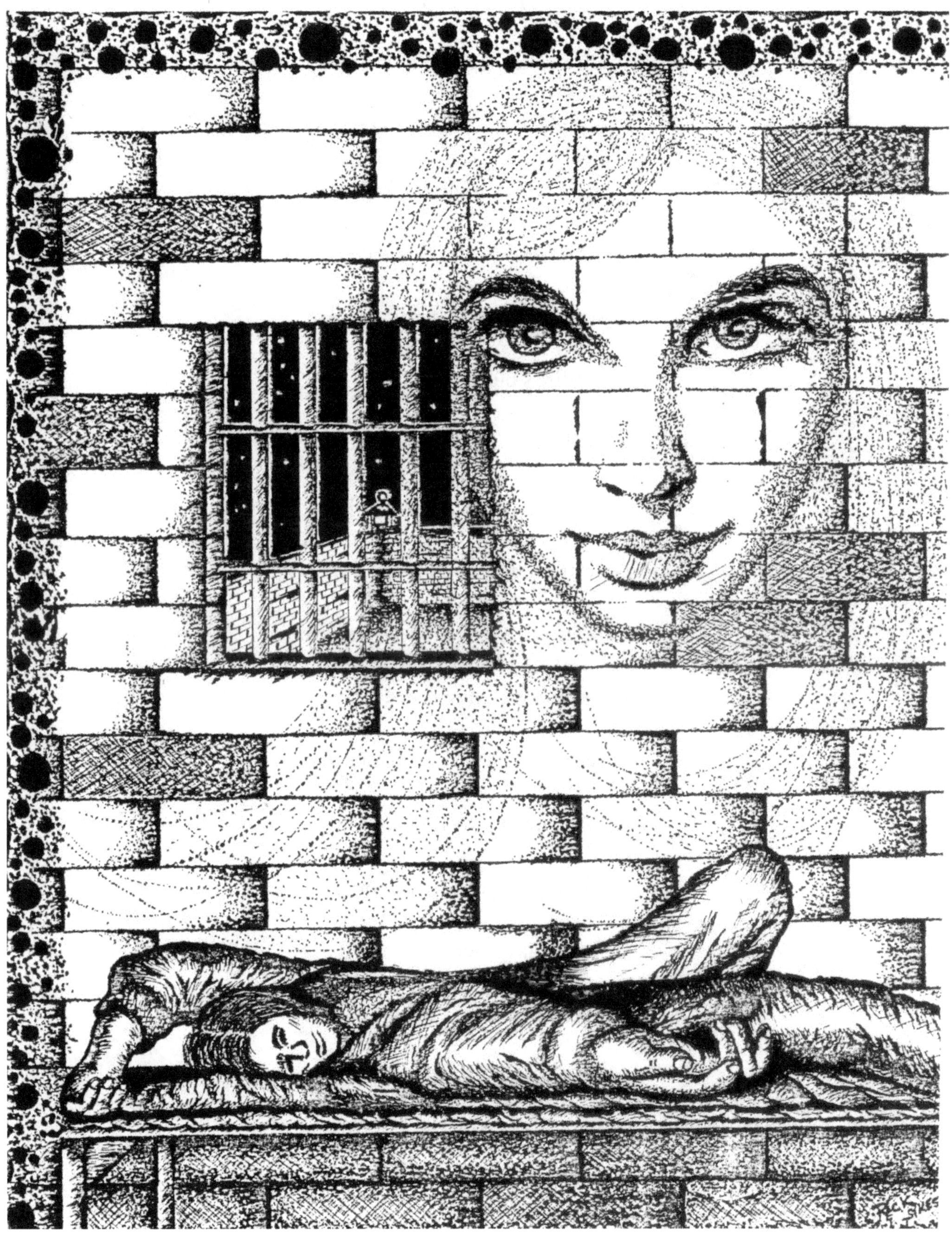

## *Angel of Night*

Few are awake, but guards in towers

In solitude of early morning hours

You come every night without fail

To lie beside me in my cell

Answering a lonely man's prayer

Making life's burdens easier to bear

Sharing loving moments until dawn

The sweetest by far this day has known

Tenderness, peace and joy you give

Loving encouragement, desire to live

Bringing hope, rhyme and reason

Dissipating gloom and doom of prison

Tasting your lips, feeling your hand

Every need you understand

The world revolves around you

All the compassionate things you do

You cuddle me into slumber tight

To return tomorrow, my Angel of Night

## *The Dream*

I dreamed I was out of prison last night
The long awaited time to set things right
You were a picture of loveliness in my sight
For hours we kissed, as I held you tight
Soaring, orbiting the heavens, souls in flight
No windows barred in this world of sunlight
Tears of joy did I weep
So happy, I couldn't go back to sleep
I thought of a rose, though the prison yard is deep in snow
Feeling great, awakening from a beautiful dream, you know
It seemed that I had touched you, it was grand
Tenderness of your eyes, caress of your loving hand
Tasting of honey were your sweet lips
My eyes traced your soft body like finger-tips
You snuggled up to me so warm, so mine
These moments totally divine
No light, no dark, no time, in this dream of ours
Filled of love scents and of wild-flowers
Talking of the many things we'll do
My antics bringing gay laughter to you
Smiling, drifting into sleep; cuddled, you and me
Sailing peacefully into tomorrow's reality

## *Portrait of My Golden Girl*

Finest tints of white-yellow closing the day

Accents of vivid orange, arrays of scarlet's bold display

Streamlets of colors that seem to say

I am yours echoes on silver shafts and vertical ray

Horizons ablaze, bathed with your golden hue

Continually changing, fresh and new

Suspended splendor in globe of my favorite blue

Spellbound in repetition, I whisper, "I love you"

In sad profusion I watch your glorious retreat

Yet, darkness hides not memories sweet

Distorts not enchantment complete

Seeking vengeance, before dawn, to lie night slain at your feet

Threshing wrathfully, I hunt the abode of darkness

In agony tumbling in horrid pits, until night is gone

A faint glow in the east, proclaiming the quarry has flown

I'll rest from sunrise, 'til you come for our moment alone

## *My Little Dream*

Since skies were blue, I have loved you

Long before nights faded into day

Longer than tomorrows have been new

Before children learned to play

I loved you before buttercups painted meadows yellow

Leaves whispered wind refrains

Before colors and songs became gay and mellow

And roses were kissed by gentle rains

Even before stars thought to shine

Cool springs flowed to the rippling stream

The Master designer made you mine

To love forever, my little dream

## *Image of Memory*

In the shadowy doorway an eerie glow

The image of a girl I knew years ago

Memories linger haunting my mind

She loved me, but I treated her unkind

When I'm alone, she appears, to my surprise

I see the hurt and loneliness in her eyes

My mind is playing tricks on me

Yet, I do so plainly see

She beckons tenderly with loving hands

Smiling sweetly, her hair like desert sands

I reach out to touch her, but no one is there

Awakened I see upon my pillow, a strand of golden hair

Stumbling through day, hiding from night

Wondering if memory can become reality

Wishing that somehow it might

If it can't be, perhaps I'll become memory

Then follow my dream to eternity

Into the sea, into the sea

## *To An Angel*

Last night an Angel came on silver wings

She spoke of roses, tomorrows, love, and things

Thoughts that haunt a lonely man's dreams

She wrote beautiful, cherished lines

I want you, need you, you are the sun that shines

On one page alone, she wrote 'I love you' seven times

Saying, my life is empty since you are gone

Yet, I feel you near, though I am alone

I will be so happy when you come home

Blossoms are on the forsythia and dogwood tree

I saw a Robin...Spring is near...I want you with me

Remember I love you...as if I could forget her

She brightens my spirits and I feel much better

When my angel visits me, even if only in a letter

## *Empty Dawn*

I dreamed I awoke and found you gone,

I felt lost and so alone.

Somehow something is all wrong!

Uneasy feelings like a sad, sad song.

Sometimes, love just can't grow.

It withers and dies, painfully slow.

When there is nothing left inside,

Nothing can revive loves that's died.

If you're bound for leaving, tell me so.

Don't slip away when you go.

Look into my eyes, and then I will know,

For, sadly the truth will show.

I feel happiness has flown,

And sorrow rides the empty dawn.

## *So Very Often*

Sunset has faded golden

Over sea and mountains blue

The best part of the day has come

So very often, all night through

Thinking of you warmly

While nightfall is new

And hoping that Angels

Bring happiness to you

Softly whispering a reminder

That one as loved as you

Is dreamed of with affection

So very often, all night through

Sleep peacefully, lovely lady

Fairest of roses true

We will wander through dreamland

So very often, all night through

## *You and Abilene*

Dream tripping, I see streets shining with rain

It seems so long that we have been parted

Wondering, if you are as lovely as you used to be

I was so proud to take you places with me

Not a moment of life was wasted

Laughter and tears we tasted

That old flame still burns brightly

I review and renew yesterday's passions nightly

I wonder how it will be

When at last I am free

Will I be welcome in the old town?

Will you still want me around?

Just what will be the scene

When I return to you and Abilene?

# PRISON YARD

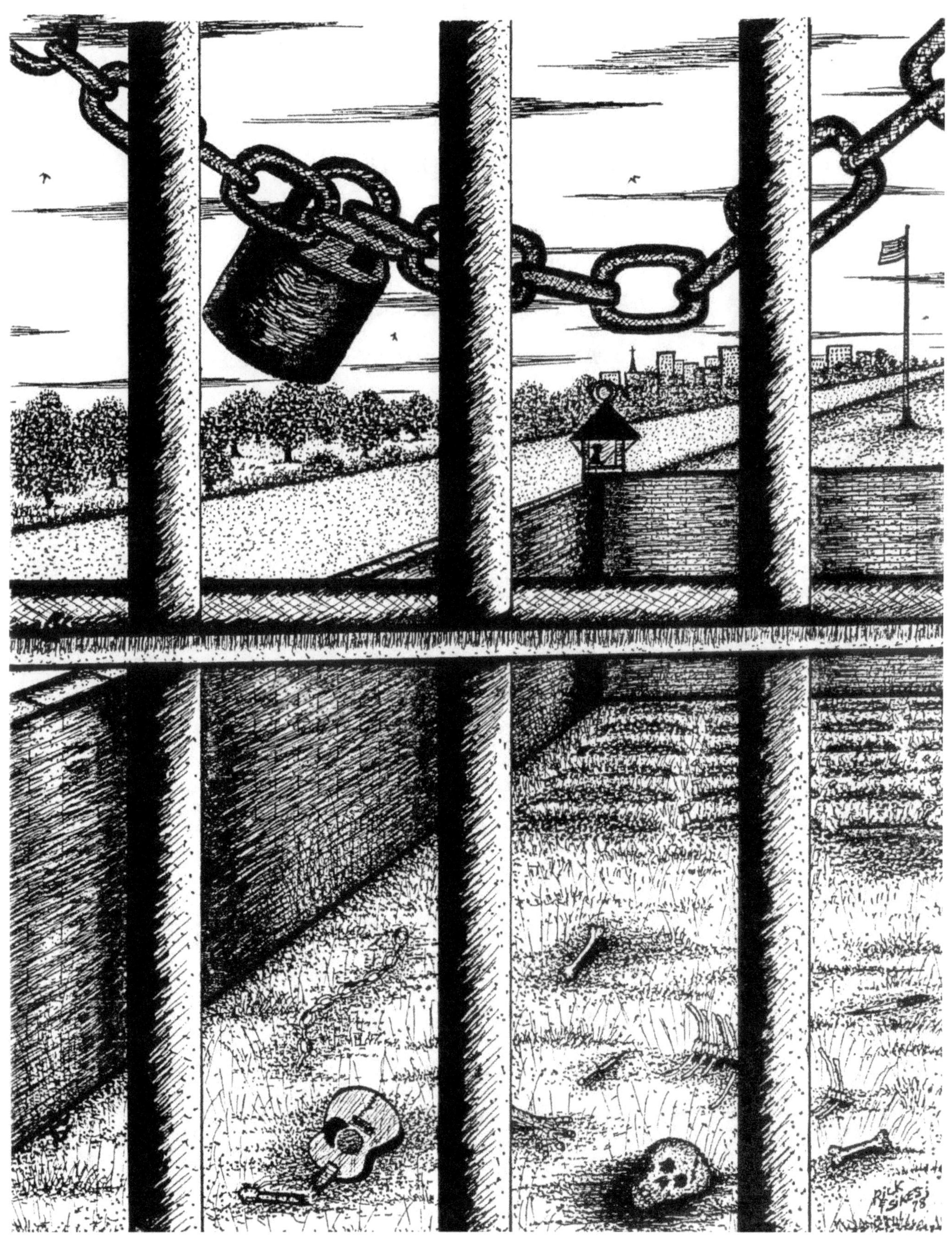

## *All American Prison Scene*

This ain't just another tale
Of losers and boozers
And people who have been in jail.
There are stories about prisons,
Songs about seasons.
This is one about time,
And lots of folks reasons.
You begin to realize time has flown,
When you ponder whereabouts
Of those you have known.
Mack, went from Marion to marrying.
And Juan back to San Antone.
Bill, left Leavenworth, headed for Fort Worth.
Old Frank just went on home.
Jack, went from Huntsville to Nashville.
Joe left Quentin, dreaming of Barbi Benton.
Pete, from Joliet, to his loving wife Juliet,
But, she's living with Jody.
That'll be a surprise, I bet!
Some have gone from bad to worse.
Some left in limousines,
Others left in a hearse.
Some left broke, some in style.
I haven't gone anywhere,
But I've been gone a long while.

Charlie left Tucker to become a trucker.
Tony left Angela, became a Holy-Roller.
Quit raising hell, started raising kids.
Others out the gate of prison,
Straight to the back alley skids.
Tom had this money lust.
Bob had a dope bust.
Andy went from rags to riches.
But only for a little while.
He's back in Cook County waiting for trial.
Jim didn't do much time.
Was what they call a white-collar crime.
Ripped-off a few million bucks.
Another politician
Trying to make an honest dollar.
From the poor-house to the big-house,
A very common style.
From bumming to slumming,
A good ol' boy goes wild.
Freedom to boredom, few stops between.
A slice of life and current theme
The 'all American prison scene'.

## *Prison Reason*

Fate seems to fall upon some less fortunate men
To bear most of the nation's hostility and sin
Public example for the citizen to see
Though the onlookers be more guilty than he
Saying they will help, even teach a trade
All the while, trying to destroy dignity and pride, of which men are made
Taking their freedom, hiding them from the eyes of society
Demanding and crushing, these tyrants almighty
Year after year, since time began, crime rates have risen
Supposedly creating need for incarcerations in prison
Hundreds of thousands, tossed into the penal cesspools
Cloaked in bitterness, educated well in criminal training schools
The hard working, honest tax-payer must pay, for every day
The prisoner must stay, while both lives are drifting away
Wasting money, wasting time, such a useless combination
Bringing much sorrow and no rehabilitation
Targeted for abusive whims and sadistic discriminations
Outrageous prices for cruel, unfruitful isolations
Tell me, so that I may understand then
In what ways does this benefit or contribute to creative men?

## *Where Lonely People Go*

Drink too much, they've been in jail.
Lives of trouble and mistakes
Dwelling in living hell.
No stranger to heartaches,
Never letting feelings show,
You find them out on a limb,
Where lonely people go.
Hiding tears from their eyes,
Lashing out in their pain,
Keeping hearts in disguise,
So they won't be hurt again.
That's the way life is; it is so.
Whatever the name,
That is the game,
Where lonely people go.
Lighted bright or dim,
Music soft or loud,
Chances are slim,
Fitting into the crowd.
Tempo fast or slow,
It's never mattered.
For dreams are shattered,
Where lonely people go.

## *Changing Times*

Folks been saying ever since I've been around
"Look up." So, I lifted my eyes from the ground
The most I've been up, is the bottom side of down
I guess from the top, they can't see the bottom
They can't sing the blues, if they ain't got 'em
Poor folk's money won't buy very much
Freedom has no meaning, when there is no such
Hard times don't have a gentle touch
Minds wander in dreams, bodies are bound
Hearts can't lay down the beat, without sound
Common folks have no right to things or craves
Because a few are masters, many are slaves
Games called inflation, starvation, recession
Work, sweat, be cursed and damn your impression
It's hell to pay, if you buck oppression
Times ain't gonna be like they've been before
Courage has been knocking at poor folk's door
Hungry children crying, brings resolution
Time will come when men will be men
Times will change, we will be free again

# *Lament To Failure*

In the most secretive hiding places,

Truth finds me there.

I close my eyes, not wishing to see,

For when I focus upon reality,

I do not perceive what I want to be.

Closing my mind and ear,

Truth I wish not to hear.

Even so, for as long as I run,

It shall be, I will never be,

I am the great deceiver

Of none, but me.

Sad to say, I am a failure,

Even at self deceit.

"Pertinent to the quality of the work, is the genuine interest and love of the work. Let each find individual preferences; encourage them to pursue these interests, therefore producing dedicated and creative workers in all fields, to become the ultimate experts."

Rick Sikes

## *Small Sacrifices*

That bird in the sky is free

Just like me, he is flying

That's smog in his eye, he's not crying

Because birds don't cry

We have a lot in common

I really don't know what

We neither are especially attractive

But we are both radioactive

If I wasn't choking, I'd be joking

Freedom pollution is what we've got

We dine on artificial fodder

Drink vintage re-cycled water

That's how we dine, our fare is fine

Since we are free you see

We are both endangered members

Like strip-mine timbers

Not likely to grow, but we know

It's so, if we should go

It will be in the best of interest

Of progress and technology

A small price, you'll agree

Do not mourn, be sad and forlorn

Blast the factories whistles and horn

A final goodbye to that bird and I

For the nation, in the name of patriotic contamination

A small sacrifice, that bird and me

It's worth it all, we recall - to be free

# *Nothing More*

Such honor have I for your love
To be the one you chose
Thoughts of you leave me in ecstasy
And want of compose
You are a radiant beauty
Shaming the loveliest rose
Awakening new emotions
Heights of passion grows
Your eyes have a magical twinkle
Sparkling charm invariably shows
Moods are lighter
All about you brightly glows
Currents of warmth
Sweet peace around you flows
Blue skies prevail
Darkness goes
To explain the feeling
My heart knows
I can only say, it's love
Nothing more, I suppose

## *Ballad For An Imaginary Movie Queen*

You got me wrong, I'm not a stage.

But, if you're gonna act, act your age!

A bad show from the start,

Cue-card lines, not from the heart.

The plot is cold, the music wrong,

Worn out story, same ol' song.

You can tell your scriptwriter

I am a lover, not a fighter!

These scenes are re-runs of my past,

Follies with an all-loser cast.

Fancy yourself in the limelight,

On that gala opening night.

In the truth of the final scene,

You will see just what I mean.

You're not a leading lady; it's only your notion.

Be ready to roll 'em with plenty of emotion.

Sorry, but life is just that way.

I won't play any bit parts in the play.

## *The Make*

Somewhere between lust and love,

She'll find what she's thinking of.

Another one night stand with any man,

She'll take what he's giving.

That's her way of living.

She's on the make.

Her smile says she's on the take.

Her eyes say she's an easy make.

She knows how it's always been

She wants it to be the same again.

She's on the make.

She's easy without shame,

Not trying to refrain.

Anything to fulfill,

Claiming the moment's thrill.

She'll go at the mention

For, she craves attention.

She's on the make.

## *Liberation-Damnation*

They say women's liberation,

Is changing the nation.

Things being as bad as they are.

From pressing your suits,

To polishing your boots,

Then lighting your cigar.

I dream of the good ol' days,

The best times by far.

When women were women,

And men didn't try to be.

Where women are women,

And men are glad they are.

Do you have any other wishes,

When I've finished with the dishes?

The kids are confused, for them it's hard.

So would you not be mad,

If they just call you Dad,

While I sleep with the dog in the yard?

# *My Gal Suzie*

I've found the one of my dreams

There can be no other

I loved her always it seems

She's a friend and a lover

A lady, and I don't mean maybe

You'd see why I'm choosy

Why I call her my baby, if you knew Suzie

Just playing around

I met Betty, Janie, and Mary

Before I settled down

There was Linda, Pat, and Sherry

They were cute and neat

And in all their special ways, sweet

We sure had a ball in this whole world

There isn't any doubt it's the greatest girl

I'm talking about - singing a happy tune

None sad or bluesy - 'cause I hung the moon

For my gal Suzie

## *Right Woman, Wrong Man*

John had a few acres down in the holler
Worked like hell for a poor man's dollar
His only pleasure and treasure in life
Was a pretty young blond-haired wife
She had big-blue eyes, those eyes did talk
Men hungered just watching her walk
She a beauty, he was rough and tan
A delicate flower, a mountain man
From the city, came a man one day
Strip-mine locations to survey
John's wife thought the dandy a cutie
He was awed by the stunning native beauty
Instantly, seems an affair was prime
They didn't tarry nor waste any time
For soon was conceived a cheating plan
A ripe woman and her lover man
In their passion, they were overzealous
Neglecting that John was insanely jealous
Jealousy will drive some out of their mind
John was precisely that kind
Death stalked those peaceful hills
And ended their lives and the plan
Of the right woman and the wrong man

## *Bringing It In*

Been happening since time began,

Anything so fine can't be sin.

Mill is grinding, the gin is gonna' gin,

So come on, start bringing it in.

Things are better than they've ever been.

There's been a big change in trend,

Bikinis and sunshine are in style again.

The good times are here, amen!

Happiness is blowing in the wind,

People are bringing it in.

Women are showing more interest in men.

They got a hungry look,

And it ain't for just a friend.

They are ready to go

And most have already been,

Bringing it in.

# THE TOWER

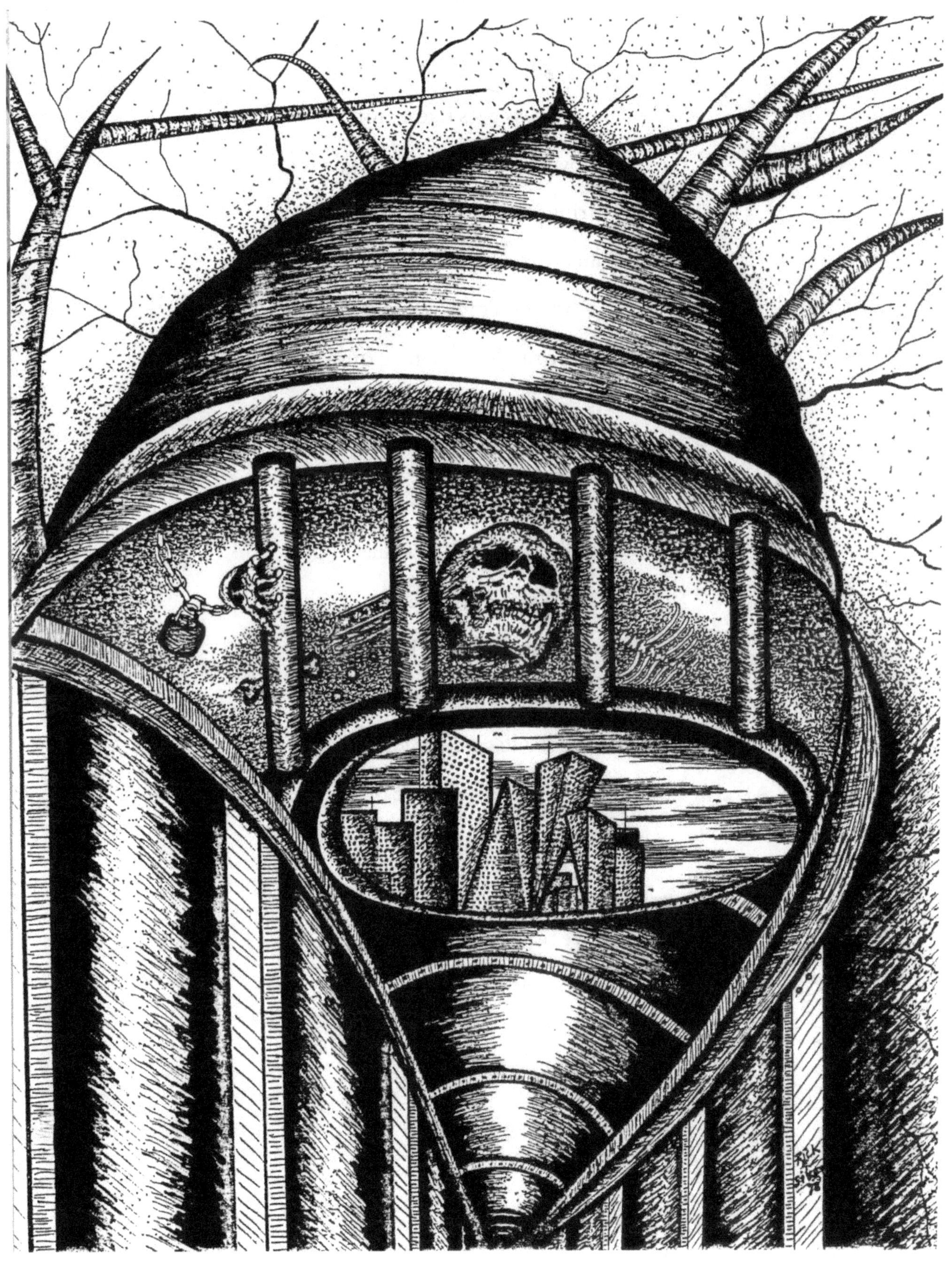

## *The Final Hour*

Long nights melt into morning,
Loneliness cuts like a knife.
Knowing that the dawning,
Brings one less day of life.
I can't undo what I have done,
And I don't want to die.
But the race will soon be run,
As the moments swiftly fly.
If I could start my life anew,
Many changes I'd make.
But payment is now due,
For my one last mistake.
In the silence of these final hours,
No one can know the remorse I bear.
There are no cards or flowers,
For there is none to care.
No bells tolling in the tower,
When they strap me in the chair.
I have reached the final hour.
Right or wrong, it all ends here.

## *I, The Intruder*

On Monday, I awoke to the gentleness of a mother's love

Tuesday, I began to discover wonders of earth and heavens above

Then, Wednesday I was caught in youth's magic spell

Thursday, adulthood found me, thoughts too many to tell

Another kind of love came Friday, fragile as a rose

Her sweetness, the softness of secrets we shared, only heaven knows

Saturday, sands of time foretold the coming conclusion

In dignity, I humbly acknowledged my intrusion

Early Sunday morn, I head distant mission bells ringing

Followed a pathway to a glen far away, where angels were singing

For a moment, I shared those emotions of happiness and of strife

Was a player in the games of mortals, called life

For me, the mysteries of the ages are no longer hidden

But, for such as I, intrusion is forbidden

## *In The Name of Justice*

The crowd gathered in hostile violence

Enforcers of law stood by in silence

The lash whistled then sounded a crack

Leather tore flesh upon his back

He stumbled but shed no tears

In a barrage of insults and jeers

The crowd raged in animosity

Looking on in wild curiosity

Theirs was thirst for blood to slake

Enjoying cruelty for cruelties sake

Public demand not to be satisfied

Until the accused pleaded and cried

They would break him with punishing blow

Until he cried out mercy to show

No cry came, nor not one plea

No such pleasure the mob did see

Angrier they grew waiting repentance to hear

For their prisoner, no punishment too severe

The flogger quickened his pace

The wrath of hell upon his face

Then he lightened just a measure

Else death might rob their pleasure

The prisoner bound tight was reeling

Stumbled but showed no feeling

"Let us see blood! Let us see bone!"

The raging mass raved on

Again and again the lash tore

The madness shouted, "More, more!"

Frenzied tempo rose in insane hate

The prisoner fell as if by fate

His agony was imagined not known

For his consciousness was gone

They shouted with wicked glee

For what was yet to be

No heartfelt compassion's tug

They were self righteous hypocrites, smug

They vented their own guilt and fears

For their secret sins over the years

To pacify nagging consciences somehow

They were righting their wrongs now

And after the blood lust has died

To reason I could not save him if I tried

Then the prisoner slightly stirred

They took up chanting the condemning word

Shouting in unison with each breath

"Death – death – death – death!"

The dying man looked into crazed, hate-filled eyes

Moaned, "Thank God only once a man dies."

The body fell limp as blood began to flow red

It was over for the soul had fled

The mob slowly parted and went their way

Good citizens did their duty this day

Later the truth did come to light

The man they killed was innocent and right

The good people deny the blame

And none of them accept their shame

Each one stands guilty as accused

But in the name of justice they are excused

## *Gentle Fury*

My body screams its needs in countless ways,

Pulse pounding as hot blood surges fast

Burning flesh tingles for your hungry lips

Each finger aching, throbbing for the silken touch of you

Beyond bounds of reasoning the wanting grows

Fiery, longing, raging, writhing, deep within

Seeking to draw of you, to drink deeply

For you are the essence, the nectar of love I crave

My lips anticipating claiming your velvet body

Seizing the abundant and apparent desires

Yielding honey - sweet, warm honey

No bars shall prohibit our needs

No strange, foolish morality will starve our greed

Wishing to fill every need you may express

Fully responding, body and soul

Controlling my being above, beyond and below

In any, every capacity, your passions hold

In tender violence, to explore and probe

Until calm, peace and satisfaction consumes our souls

## *Just Wanna Be Gone*

I woke up feeling bad, I ain't no place

Ain't the first time I had that feeling

No use talking about a done-run race

Kisses ain't all that woman is stealing

She don't mind who she is hurting

With bedroom eyes and flashing smile

She is always slipping and flirting

A man-hungry look and about half wild

I don't care where I go, just wanna be gone

My hat is on and I grabbed my bag

These ain't my ol' boots I got on

Thumb me a ride away from this drag

I like the feeling of knowing

I don't care if I am wrong

At last I'm finally going

I just wanna be gone

## *Museum Of Memory*

They are here and there,

Thanks to you they're everywhere.

Stacked from ceiling to floor,

I can hardly live here anymore.

Into my life they've crowded,

Until my heart is shrouded,

In this museum of memory.

The pictures of perfection,

Are your special section.

Beauty captures the eye.

So it's no wonder why,

You are sweetest my pleasure.

My greatest treasure,

In this museum of memory.

# *I Can*

You ask why I sit alone
And seem so lonely
Perhaps you'll understand
It's not an uncommon story
About a woman and a man
Anyone can tell it...I can
Names and games
Faces and places
Smiles and frowns
On merry-go-rounds
Players on the field
Spectators in the stand
If anyone can know
The length of the row...I can
A little trying, some crying
Love that is dying
Without plot nor plan
People with names
Playing parts over again
Anyone can act the role...I can

# *A LITTLE GIRL AND BOUQUET OF ROSES*

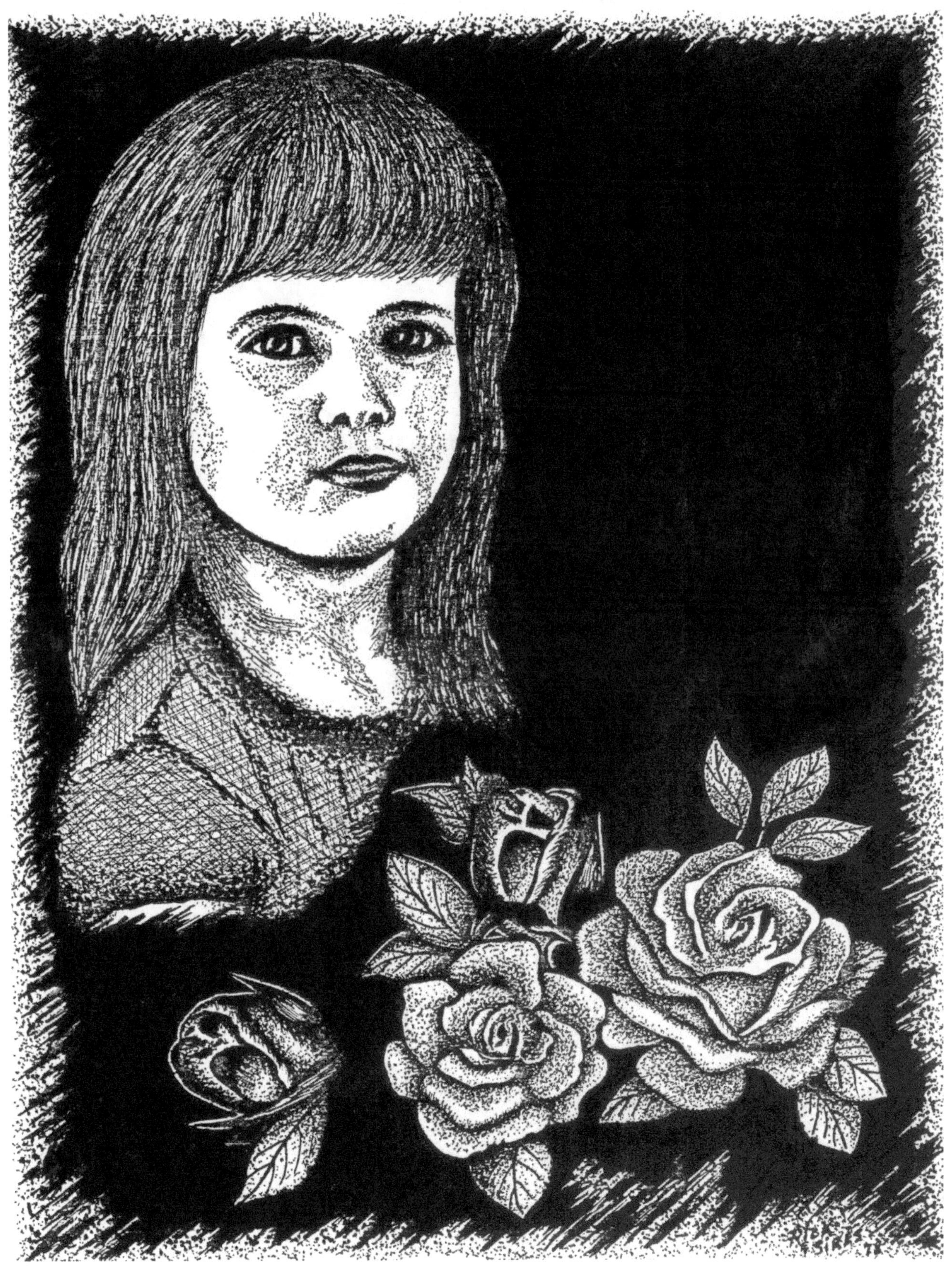

## *Little Girls and Roses*

Roses are like pretty little girls

Petals swirling, lovely curls

Sweetly blushes the scented roses

Angel cheeks, buds like little noses

Tender fragile blooming at random

Prettiest ones are where you find them

Dew kissed angels from above

Rare beauties symbols of love

Delicate and soft seem they fantasy

Charming warmth assures reality

Thankful am I that both grows

Pretty little girls and the beautiful rose

## *Winter Roses*

Like a winter rose

When petals fall one by one

I lost you day by day

Being too wrong too long

Oh foolish things I've done

You tried and cried

'Til everything died

Like the warm summer sun

Love faded slowly away

Leaving me to regret

One I am never to forget

Mourning in sad repose

A dying winter rose

How it hurts to know love is dying

Like a winter rose, it just can't be

I keep telling me

Losing you hopelessly

Like a winter rose

# No, No, Never

Rivers flowing seemingly forever

To never run dry

We should always be together

Yes, you and I

Lie in my arms, peacefully sleep

If bad times come by

The willows may weep

You will have no reason to cry

You won't feel alone and lost

Nor know the chill of loneliness' frost

Our love will not die

Nor take wings and fly

Our heaven has just started

We will never be parted

No, No, Never!

## *The Rhyme*

I cannot express happiness in a line

For you are roses in winter time

The rainbow, moon, and stars that shine

Princess of perfection divine

Gentle, understanding, and kind

Enchantment capturing my mind

As pathways of emotion unwind

From lips intoxicating as wine

Feelings of ecstasy sublime

Reason for devoted time

Trying to compose worthy verse or line

Expressions of thankfulness that you are mine

# *WILDFLOWERS*

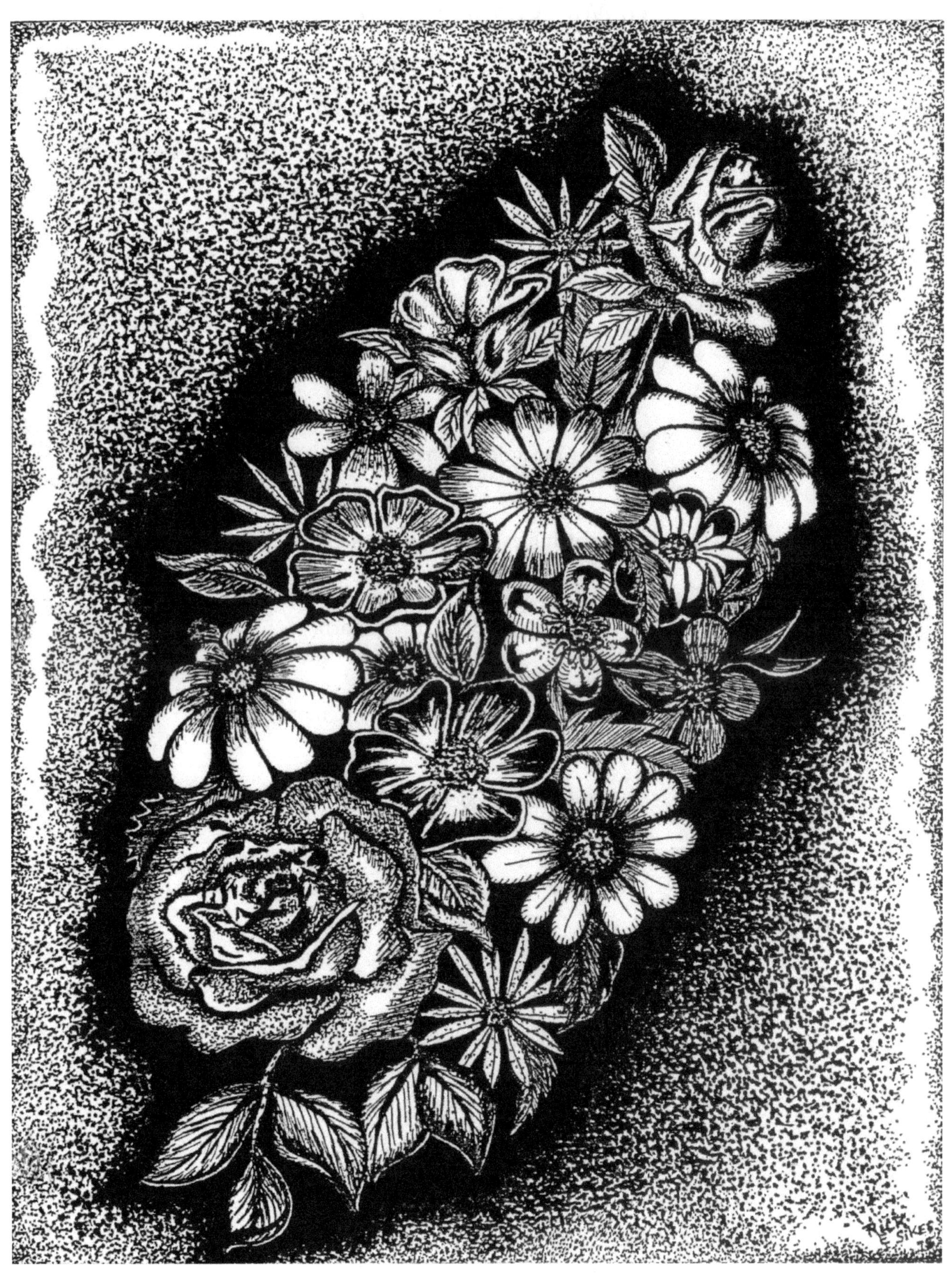

## *To My Wildflower Princess*

Love has brought a new song to sing,

As playful winds whisper of spring.

Red roses wash in morning dew,

A lovely one-of-a-kind wildflower grew.

Beauty designed by nature's art,

Capturing every eye and heart.

Before vision of earth, life is born,

Softly as dawn upon the slumbering morn.

Exotic as the poet's dreams,

Lovelier than mountains and streams.

Tolling bells of laughter ring,

Chanting joyous love on golden wing.

Enchantress of stars in twilight,

Blanket of warmth throughout the night.

Perfection mortal, truly displayed,

Flawless in bright sunlight or evening's shade.

Nothing can more intensely inspire,

Create depths of feelings and desire.

A tribute in lyric and song,

Before the wildflower princess' throne.

Heralding in the mellowing year,

Those tender moments long held dear.

Time of blessings that forever unite,

Joyously enjoined in love's delight.

## *Aster Star-Flower Daisy*

A tribute to a lovely flower

Ornate beauties have their hour

Saluting pageants nonce and past times

Honoring their presence these humble lines

Tears of beautiful Ashea, dust of the star

Fair Ariadne, lover of Theseus, slayer of Minotaur

Symbolic of the despairing Aegeus whose blood fell

Cast in sorcery of Medea's purple spell

Justly deemed sacred in noble splendor

Wreaths to decorate ancient god's altar

Legend in varied color deserving song and praises

Truly a rightful heir, Michaelmas daisies

## *Extol From Soul*

Exquisite beauty of a charming rose viewed in awe
For lust is the nature of men
Errant eyes fill with torrid dreams in fantasy
Aware that greatest beauty often lies within
Flawless perfection enhanced by her silver wardrobe of diamond dew
Lovely butterflies oft times perch as a crown for the enviable princess too
Wholly I drink of this extravaganza of petite femininity I behold
I am a native born earth man
Mundanely, my emotions unfold
Seeking, craving, endeavoring...savoring the erotic raptures
All hope lies within sincerity of her heart
For my soul she surely captures
Intimacy, delicate love scenes do not suffice
Nor does repetitious contact and fiery touch
Love must encompass the passion with hearts
For souls require much
The venture is unworthy for winnowing
Or lust seed on vanishing winds casting
Serenity prevails the winsome ensnarement
Bound fully to love everlasting

# COUNTRY

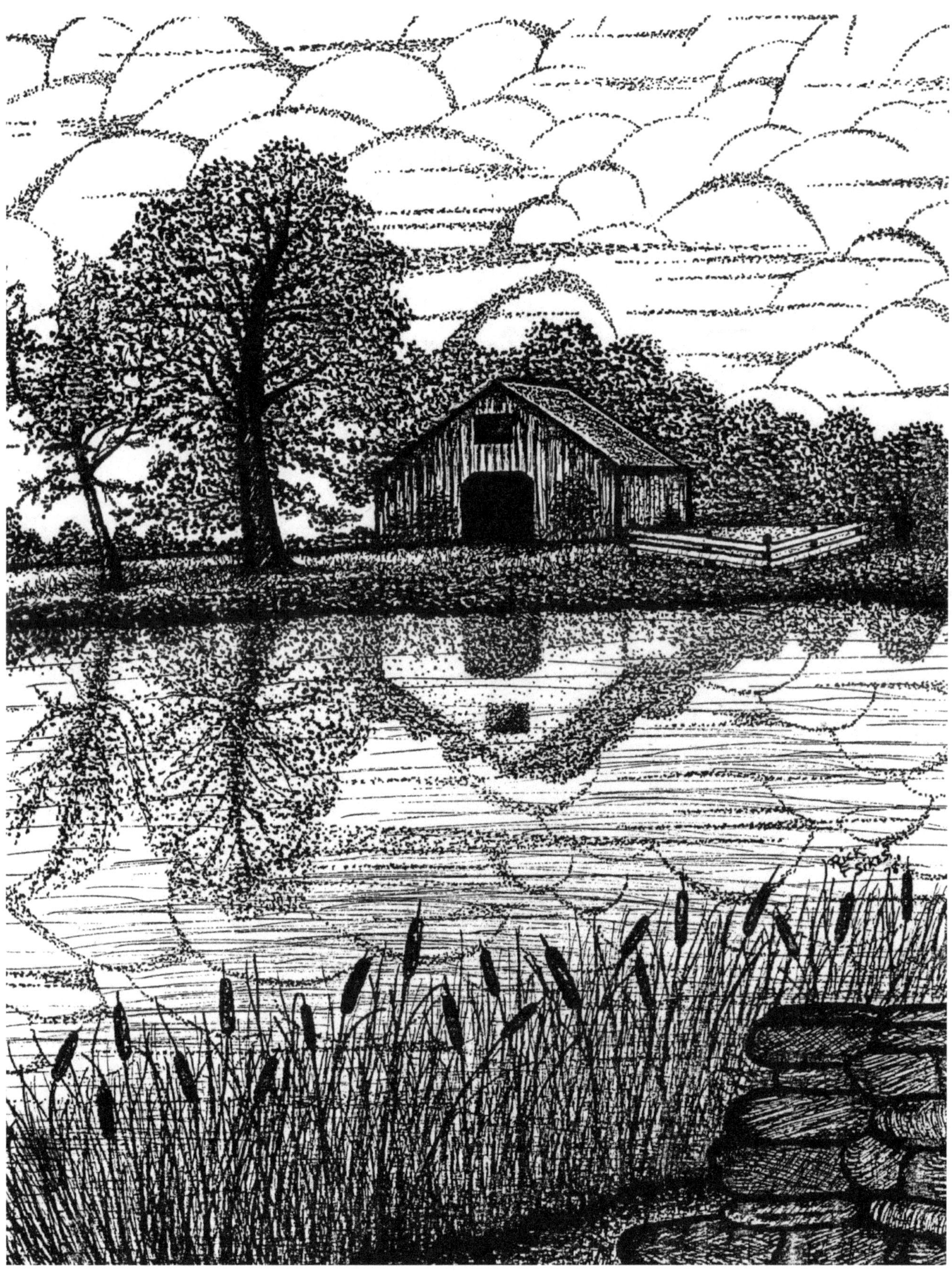

## *Country Rain*

I am longing for the

Sounds of country rain

To hush the rude noises

Of the streets

Where arrogant, urgent

Vehicles upon asphalt sheets

Drone in impatient protests

To off-keys, off-beats

In mechanical sleepless fights

I struggle with nights

Earnestly wishing again

For peaceful sounds

Of gentle country rain

## *My Leanhaun Shee*

If I gathered all the gold from the shores,

Could claim charms of finest ladies,

Know temptations of the sultriest whores,

Own acres of diamonds, brilliant as dew,

All these combined would not compare

To the wondrous lure of you.

To control the sun, moon, and mighty sea,

Would be but trivial to the thrills,

And awe that you bring to me.

Could I capture magic and melodies.

Of greatest violin and guitar?

In fascination, I would seek you,

Matters not, where you are.

Delicately you destroy body and soul,

From within, from without, yet then,

Foolishly, I would yield willingly,

Knowing that you thrive upon such men.

Devour me completely my maid of mist.

Tenderly pierce this heart, I cannot resist.

## *My Promise*

These words from my heart to you

You'll find each of them to be true

As we journey upon life's troubled seas

Our days are numbered like falling leaves

All too soon the time is gone

But, not the happiness we've known

One day you'll speak and I won't answer, hun

Then you'll know I've followed the sun

Leaving a token you'll not forget

In each brilliant Texas sunset

No need for sadness nor mournful call

Need not one tear drop ever fall

I'll never be further than your heart

For nothing shall split the two apart

When finally work on earth is done

We'll simply walk on following the sun

I know you'll follow after awhile

Then together we'll walk the golden isle

Traveling where mortals only dream of

In an eternal land of perfect love

Don't be lonely, weep nor fret

Just look toward that beautiful sunset

Knowing it has just begun

When you join me to follow the sun

We'll find that heaven is placed beyond the west

A paradise of total peace and rest

Remember each evening's amber hue

Is a renewal of My Promise to you

## *Love Venture*

So much in love we spoke, only in short sentence

Filled with new emotions, exploring ecstasy without repentance

Earth angels came from hiding and gathered in nature's chorus

The universe spread like a vast treasure chest before us

The finest vintage of love's vineyard, a delight for our taste

As we drank deeply the fleeting precious moments scurried in haste

Enchantment of spring, sultry summer flown then frost fell upon roses red

Magic and charm of the wine was gone our dashing beauty lay dormant and dead

After the dreary lingering nights, a bright new dawn came then

Joyful to be fully seasoned, knowing we'll not see yesterday again

For much in love we speak, heartedly in half sentence

Laughter rings in cheerful good times…days past receive little repentance

# *SEPARATED BY BARS*

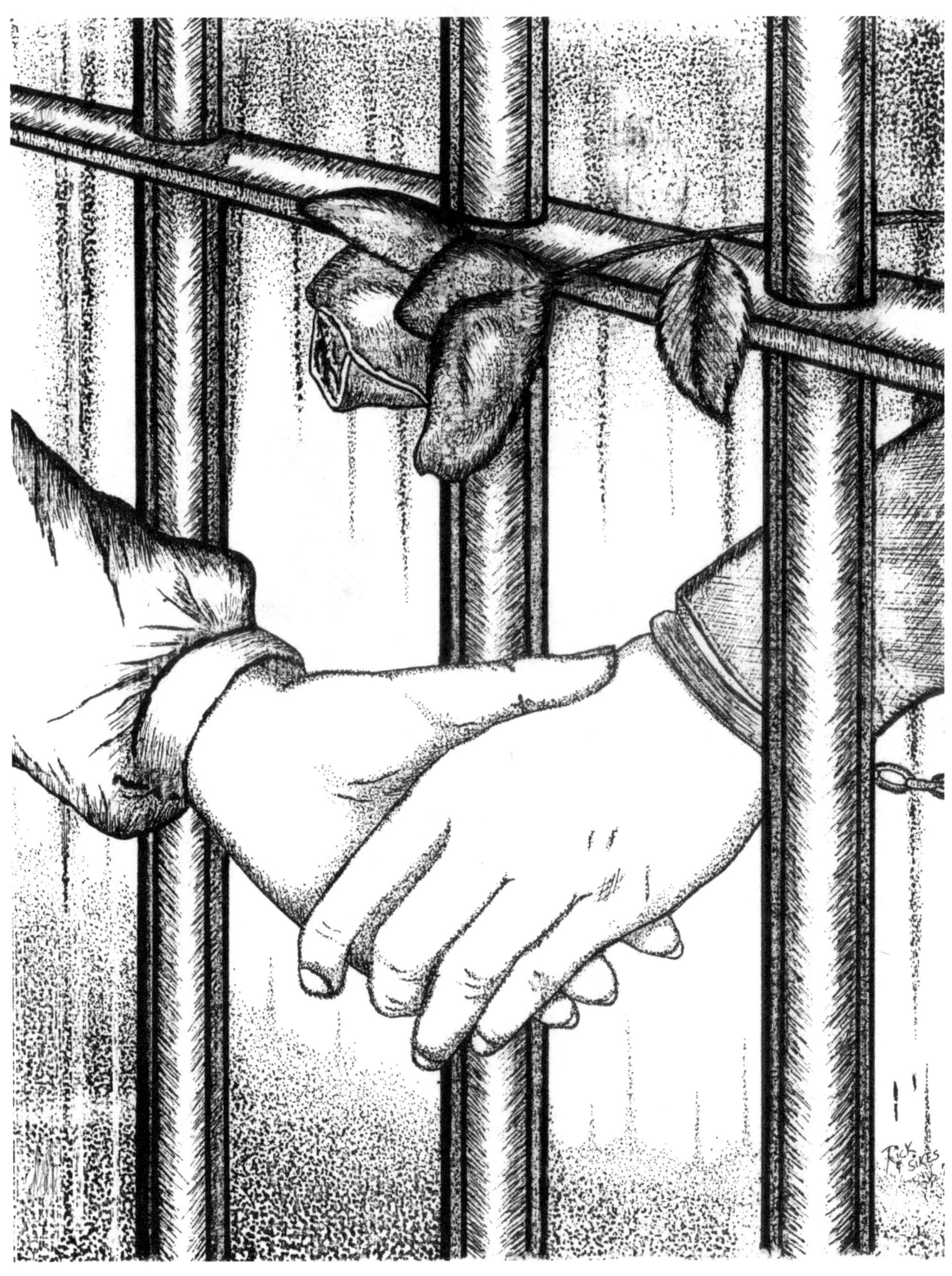

## *Just Love*

If you grow weary while waiting for me,

Remember to dream of what can be.

Hours will fly thinking of tender moments,

Sweet kisses and loving atonement.

In the morning the sun will rise in a clear sky,

After the long day sets for you and I.

I'm only a man and will probably make mistakes.

Hopefully, never one to cause heartaches.

If ever I cause one tiny tear to fall,

May it be a tear of joy; that is all.

Sorrow's shadow may not linger at our door,

Living, loving, until our time is no more.

Climbing the mountains, life's storms to weather,

You and I, hand in hand, always together.

Sharing light in darkness, bearing hard times,

Warmth in the cold, for love is divine.

Contentment, peace, confidence within,

Ours is the greatest love that has ever been!

## *Let Me Hold You*

If this old world should let you down

If you need someone who won't ask why

Come to me

Let me hold you while you cry

Let me bring you smiles

Let me bring you pleasures

Let me give love and devotion

Life's real treasures

Let me bring sunlight

To your clouded sky

Let me hold you while you cry

Come to me when dreams won't fly

When castles come tumbling from the sky

Come to me

Let me hold you while you cry

## *I Can't See The Roses*

Rain has fallen most of my years.

Sometimes I believe the sun will shine once more.

Tonight, I wonder, it just started to pour.

I can't see the roses for the tears.

The wind howls a sad melody in my ears.

Love songs and dreams are far away.

Flowers don't grow where I am today.

There are no roses, only tears.

A cloud with silver-lining never appears.

Nothing but old heartaches can I recall.

Memories, like dripping fingers of sad willows, call.

It's hard to see roses through the tears.

The sunset of eternity slowly nears.

Wrinkling youthful days with age,

Life's book ends on a final stained page.

I didn't see the roses for the tears.

## *Every Rose Has Thorns*

She goes out alone at night
I know it isn't her plan.
She does things that aren't right
I love her, I understand.
It's easy to say what you would do
Until the decision falls on you.
She don't act the way a lady should
Many say she is no good.
It doesn't matter what they say
I love that woman anyway.
She's good even though she's bad
The only real love I've had.
She's sunshine beyond dark skies
Bringing light to my dim eyes.
For me she is everything
Whatever the future may bring.
Alone in wee hours of morn
Waiting for her 'til dawn is born.
Sunrise always comes after a storm.
People talk, I hear their scorns,
But, every rose has its thorns.

# *Earth-Mates*

Disregarding imposed social values

Exploring reality in dimensions celestial

Gallant, foolish, truly beautiful

Courageous itinerants, terrestrial

Tropism begins as mortals

Search one another's eyes

Little needs to be verbally spoken

For so much they realize

Intriguing souls brought

Together at the precise time

For which fate has already

Made her invariable design

Enraptured in a magical

Force that thrills through

Attuned of ardor ample

Delightful trembling too

Unity of laughter and tears

Overflow of too full hearts

The Mandragora of nature

Earth-mates, playing their parts

# *SEASONS*

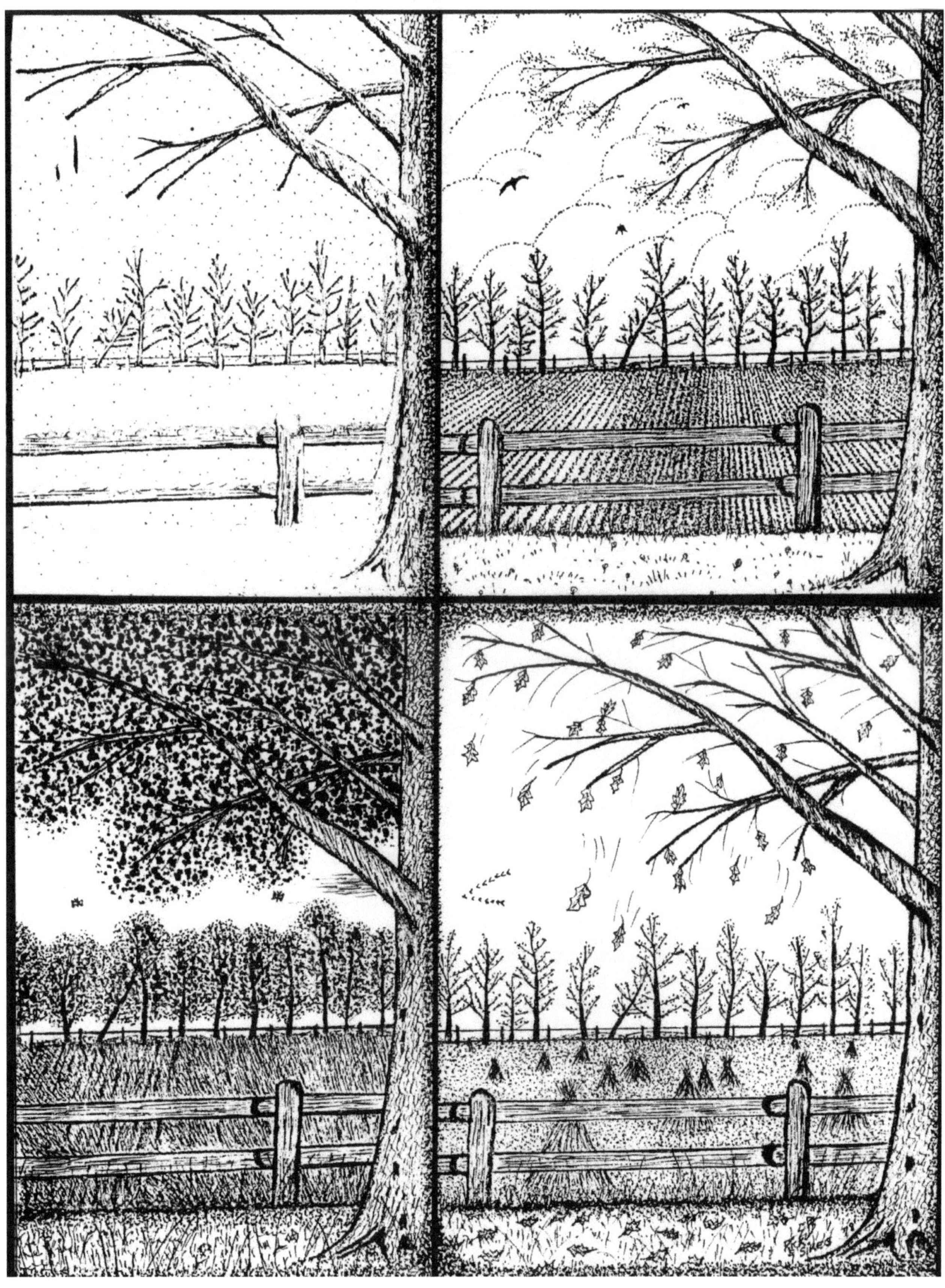

## *Reasons For Seasons*

Nature has wonderful reasons
For the changing of seasons
Wonder where one would begin
Choosing from seasons without end
Each in its own way is pleading
From the summer breeze teasing
Through autumns color display
Followed by winter's glistening way
Budding to spring's lively sight
It seems each season is really just right
Summer sweet, lazy and warm
Autumn with its lusty charm
Nothing is lovelier than the snow
Except springtime's green as things grow
Seasons were not designed in haste
They were tailored to fit every taste
Continually their acts appear
Entertaining throughout the year
One by one filling all requests
Of the seasons, I like each the best

## *After Summer - Before Winter*

Sultry summer days are almost gone

Autumn hiding places shall soon be known

Revealed by afternoon's crisp bite

Southbound geese honk in the night

Brown has replaced green of the field

Which gave winter store, a hearty yield

Trees with arms clothed orange and red

Cover earth with colorful spread

Nature's labor prevails everywhere

Preparing for winter, icy and bare

Summer fading like spring fantasy

Coming of snow restoring will be

By glowing fireside weathering the storm

New dreams for spring shall be born

## *Rainy November*

Thumbing through my memory

The same sweet one returns to me

Again, I fondly do remember

You came, bringing roses that rainy November

It should last forever

You and I being together

I think no autumn shall ever be dearer to me

Nor happier moments we will see

Pleasant recollection discloses

Vows made, sworn on the roses

Gently your ambrosial fragrance stays

Lingering through years of endless days

Moments with you were such delights

They still refresh lonely nights

Recall that moment we did realize

While looking into each other's eyes

Giving our hearts in total surrender

Was so easy, so free, so powerfully tender - On that rainy November

## *So It Is With Men*

Leaves fall, winter sets in.

Boughs, heavy with snow

Sway in forceful wind.

Rather than to break

Reluctantly, they bend.

So it is with men.

Sunset, fading purple

Into night's blend,

The day past, has been.

New dawn forever dominating

As is the ancient trend.

Perpetually changing without end.

So it is with men.

Thunderous dark clouds

Soft rains may send.

Nature, sometimes seems to be the foe,

Then next time a friend.

Taking so much from us

To return more then.

The violent destroyer

Can also tenderly mend.

So it is with men.

## *Raindrops On A Rose*

It's rainy and I'm lonely

But, I'm not the only

One who feels the same

You think of me, when it rains

Before the mistakes and tears

We shared many happy years

And love that not everyone knows

Fondly, I recall raindrops on a rose

You are not alone when you cry

I can't hide it, though I try

Friends say it shows

Especially when rain is falling on the rose

Our love is now a dying ember

Memories return to that November

The year comes and goes

And raindrops fall on the rose

## *Nature Alone*

Seeds are sown

Crops are grown

The hay is mown

Autumn is nigh, for summer is gone

Signs of frost, winter is coming on

But love lives not by seasons alone

Love is the planting in spring

Watching the growing of everything

Good yields fall harvest may bring

Love is maturing while echoes of youth yet ring

Giving of every feeling you own

But, love lives not by emotions alone

Love is the special blessing of God

God is nature, the sun, the rain, the sod

Earth is mother for all creatures to trod

Not divided, portioned by section or rod

Nature is perpetual balance, so life may go on

Love thrives only on nature alone

## *Life Can Be A Bummer*

I am just another guy,

Who is trying to get by.

I ain't bad,  ain't good,

Mostly, I'm misunderstood.

I played that patriot game, G.I. Joe,

Cowboyed in the rodeo.

Been a driver, then a thumber,

Life can be a bummer.

There are lots of good ol' boys today,

Right here in this U.S.A.

Whom trouble follows just like me,

Whatever in hell the reasons be.

If you will listen, cuz',

I'll tell you how it was.

I ran afoul of the law.

I was rolling a smoke, they saw.

They locked me in a tiny cell,

Made my life a miserable hell.

Three winters and a summer,

Life sure can be a bummer,

In a place like that,

Even if you're a real nice cat.

When I finally got out, I was flat broke.

Now let me tell you, it ain't no joke.

I didn't want to steal,

Went for days without a meal.

Finally I gave in to hunger.

Life can surely be a bummer.

Things went wrong.

Same damned song.

I'm asking you,

What's a poor boy to do?

Starve or steal?

It's that kind of a deal.

No need to guess.

The answer I'll confess.

They let the hammer down.

I'm slammer bound,

'Til sometime next summer

Life can be a bummer.

# CHRISTMAS

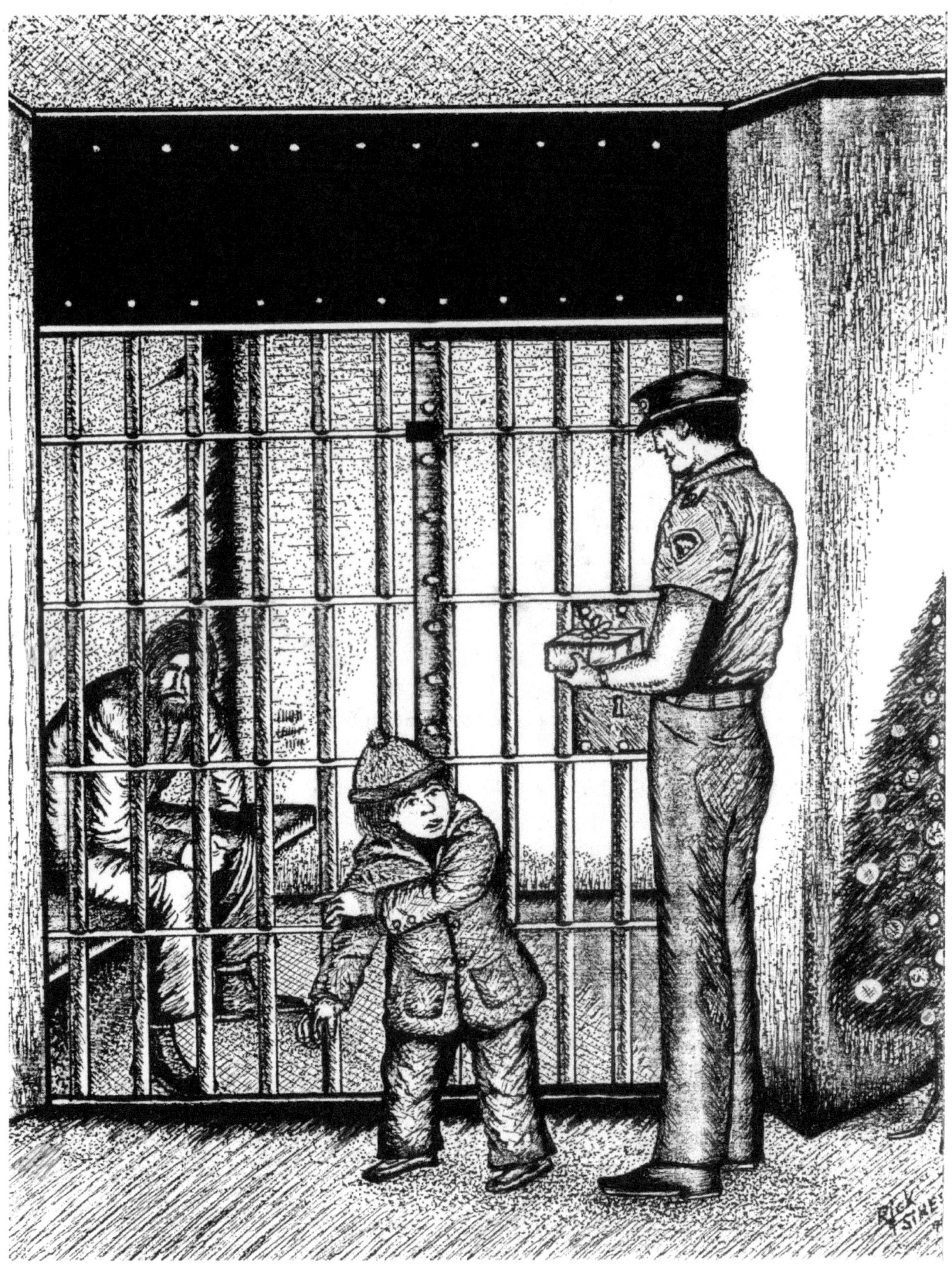

## *Old Jim's Christmas Parole*

A story of morals, for Christmas telling

Of an old convict, who next to me, was celling.

One hell of a man, that old Jim,

We called him "Pops", but all respected him.

He'd been in prison since I don't know when,

Probably chained to a tree, while they built the pen.

No one sent him anything, so we gave what we could give.

He was old and sick and had sorta' lost the will to live.

Christmas eve, he was restlessly walking,

I asked him to sit down and we started talking.

"Hell, son," he said, "I've been down roads rough and tough,

Then, I went straight, hung it up – I'd had enough.

But, you know how it is when you've fell before,

Get seen around a place where someone makes a score.

Well, that's what happened to me this time,

I got railroaded right on down the line.

I've got something in my eye, no use lying, it's a tear.

I ain't heard from my wife or kids in many a year.

But, you know boy, I got a goin' home feelin' in my soul.

Don't see how though, ain't no chance in hell for parole.

Damnedest feeling I ever had, can't understand,

Wishful thinking I reckon, of a foolish old man.

I guess you know, my home-folk passed on years ago.

It even seems if I was home, they'd be there I know,

Just like old times watching the children play.

Home is the sweetest place on earth on Christmas day.

That's something you remember, now don't forget,

I don't see no way I could get home, but it may work out yet.

Best wishes to you boy, I'm tired, gotta go to bed."

The next morning old Jim made it home, they found him dead.

## *Christmas Gift #73*

Night falls and snow drifts deep

The man stalks the halls

Turning off lights, yelling, "Go to sleep!"

Emotions run high, radios and spirits pall

Some lie awake, while hours slowly creep

Recalling fondly, the patter of little feet

Others dream of sweethearts, clutching their sheets

Daybreak finds cluttered corridors

Living-dead together, yet alone

Talking of everything and nothing - but mostly of home

Some say, "I just drove up, this is my first time."

Showing photographs of loved ones

Proudly claiming, "These are mine."

Then, there are the bitter, withdrawn

Heartbroken and the lonely-sad

Trapped in mind, chain, locks

Fences and walls, the feeling is bad

There a tear gleams on a cheek

Hopeful that no one will see

Finally, depression will overcome

Each hope of being free

Damn the righteous perfects

That caged them here

Damn their phony society and tinseled cheer

Oppression, abuse, in the name of justice?

Makes no sense to people like me

This Christmas gift from America

Rotting in their antique prisons

Nineteen-hundred seventy-three

## *Special Christmas Wish*

Slender trees appear as ebony goddess' fingers,

Spangled with a million diamonds, ice lingers.

Blue satin skies and white velvet clouds look below,

Upon an iridescent earth, a pearl of snow.

People seem different, scurrying here and there.

Unusual merriment is in the air.

Sharings of laughter and of cheer,

Brotherhood as it should be throughout the year.

From my cell window, I watch a squirrel frolic in white,

The birds flittering freely in amber sunlight.

My one special Christmas wish shall be,

For all of humanity to share this view with me.

## *Being*

Being a pessimist, I say, "I can't endure."

Being an optimist, I say, "I will, I am sure."

Being a wretch, I miserably cower.

Being noble, I stand like a tower

Being a romanticist, I feel I may cry

Being a realist, I think, "Why?"

Being a fool, I worry and wonder

Being wise, I put mental anguish asunder

Being boisterous, I yield to anger and emotion

Being humble, I seek compassion and devotion

Being insecure, I say, "The task is too hard."

Being faithful, I say, "Lead the way, I will follow, Lord."

Being a dreamer, I figured life out.

Being awakened, now I doubt.

Being that creature in the mirror I am seeing

Being just me, a human being

## *The Joy Of Christmas*

For many, life is unbearable at its best

Cruel and trying, test after test

Swiftly fate brings a sorrowful guest

Such foolish games these people play

I ponder the reason for humanity's selfish way

I wish not to spoil the mood of the holiday

For is nigh that time of year

Joyous sounds abound...Christmas is near

Mourning drowned by seasonal cheer

Tinseled sights of colors gay and glee

Gaudy reds and greens, sparkle for those who can see

For the sightless ones, it cannot be

Halls are decked with boughs of holly

Carolers sing out, so merry and jolly

For those deaf, it is all folly

Giving lavish gifts when all is still

Feasting morn through eve, gorging their fill

The hungry beg a crust of bread to be God's will

Festivities don't hide lasting social scars

Will not return loved ones lost in rich men's wars

Brings not freedom to those behind bars

The millions of sick, lonely and old

Those sleeping in the streets cold

Do they know there's joy in Christmas, or have they been told?

## *Christmas Poem For A Lady*

If I could place this poem

Beneath your Christmas tree

When you read it, if somehow

I could be there to see

Your eyes twinkling with purest love

Or even saddened with memory

You must realize that I have always

Loved you in my own sort of way

I have tried to be your knight

In armor, since first we met that day

I'd be happy to be an old rag doll

That you caressed fondly in play

I have wished your life would be filled with fun

If I shall ever behold an Angel, you are one

The gift of this poem isn't much

It doesn't have pretty wrapping and such

Just words of adoration and affection

With humble rhyming touch

No glittering red bows

Nor bright green band
Feelings from the heart of a simple man
The best of what I have to give
Please try to understand
It is true that I am a bit soiled
Somewhat faded, tattered and worn
But, if you clutch me fondly
To your breast, on Christmas morn
I will know that I bring you cheer
And I will proudly wear upon my cheek
A sparkling-silver tear
Giving me courage for the tasks
Before me, in the coming year

## *Enroute To Rendezvous*

A tattered but manumitted traveler upon the long pathway of life, the unknown

Determined, this curious earth creature immature, yet fully grown

Wholly drinking of nature, mountains, forest, desert, meadow and stream

Pursuing a reality that lies well hidden within an elusive dream

Seeking that which makes him complete, the sweetest of the vine

Hearing, seeing, feeling, learning, drifting with the tide and time

Carving, molding, building, seeking wisdom along the way

Gathering treasures hard earned, to share one special day

Acres of satin in countless shades of meadow greens and forest hue

Bountiful diamond spangled roses with dew, accented by velvet sky blue

All people of earth have these seen, but he brings these gifts to you

No strange words to speak, nor none new, yet his voice rings them true

Bringing all that mortals possess and what more the gods give

His life, past, present, and future to share and with you alone to live

Where does the poor weary vagabond find a happy melody?

One note from yesterday - one from today - the rest from destiny

In darkness he has stumbled and oft times fell

Slept on silken beds with Queens one night, the next in a prison cell

Where he has been matters not, where he is going, he alone knows

Surely a special place, lovely garden of paradise, his eyes twinkle and glow

Oh, but another, yes that elusive dream, how well is she aware

He has traveled long and hard, while patiently she awaits him there

Seasons past brought the wealth of a kingdom to their store

Tested and tried by the time, proving worth of love even more

Passing days in golden sunset or pending dawn brings them nearer

Knowing without words spoken, makes hearts dearer

The valleys and glen echo gaily with the wayfarer's happy tune

That same melody entertains far away, where a beautiful flower is soon to bloom

A song? More than a song. The sounds of love on a wing of a white Dove

The traveler coming to find reality with an elusive dream...a rendezvous of love.

## *Spawn Of Nature*

I am a child of nature, the wind

Playful breeze, furious gale

Son of soil, sky, and sun

Dusty, parched, dry desert hell

Green, entangled, swampy marsh

Lazy, flowing river in warm sunlight

Roaring, treacherous, muddy beast

Angrily lashing into dark night

I am one of many sounds

Birdsongs, soft, sweet, gentle charm

Whispering leaves and slow rain

Gruff thunder rumbling alarm

I am of every mood of nature

A part of the entire earth

A simple creature seeking survival

Traits instilled from birth

## *Self Fusion*

I'm looking for tomorrow,
Far from sadness and sorrow.
Perhaps a secluded tropical bay,
To lie in the sand watching seagulls play.
Or a cabin in the mountains high,
Where one can almost touch the sky.
Somewhere the sun surely shines,
Away from troubles and hard times.
To be accepted as I am,
Find someone who gives a damn.
Where I won't have to be tree-top tall,
Live and let live, that is all.
Get myself together and do some living.
There's a lot inside that I want to be giving.
Over a hill or around a bend,
Someplace where I fit in.
Upon the seas or desert bare,
I'll be contented breathing freedom's air.
Weary of confusion and running blind,
Time is at hand to anchor my mind.
To become one with people and the land,
Touch and be touched by friendly hand.

## *Life And Love*

Life, is one of nature's most beautiful sights to behold

From happy sunrises pink to memorial sunset gold

Created I, awesome warmth of the magic realm of love

Elusive autism, passion flowing as if from a source above

Sprinkled generously upon the planet with care

In areas obviously sparse, abundant ingredients placed there

Love and life engage in delightful colossus spawn of beauty appears

A mere seed, a bud to blossom, or to perish in tears

Applications of love's warmth and light does nourish

In full vitality and life the bloom will flourish

One fool alone would such balanced perfection destroy

Man, in ignorance, of the necessity of his disposable toy

## *Our Journey*

It is a long way from

Yesterday until tomorrow

Today is between, perhaps

Bringing happiness or sorrow

Yesterday's sunset carried it

Into memory nostalgic

Today is total reality

Tomorrow is dream-magic

The future is that day

For which we strive and seek

We reach to borrow from it

Hopeful, we positively speak

Feelings are warm and real

Looking back, side by side

Boldly facing each day

Entering tomorrow with pride

# CONVICT

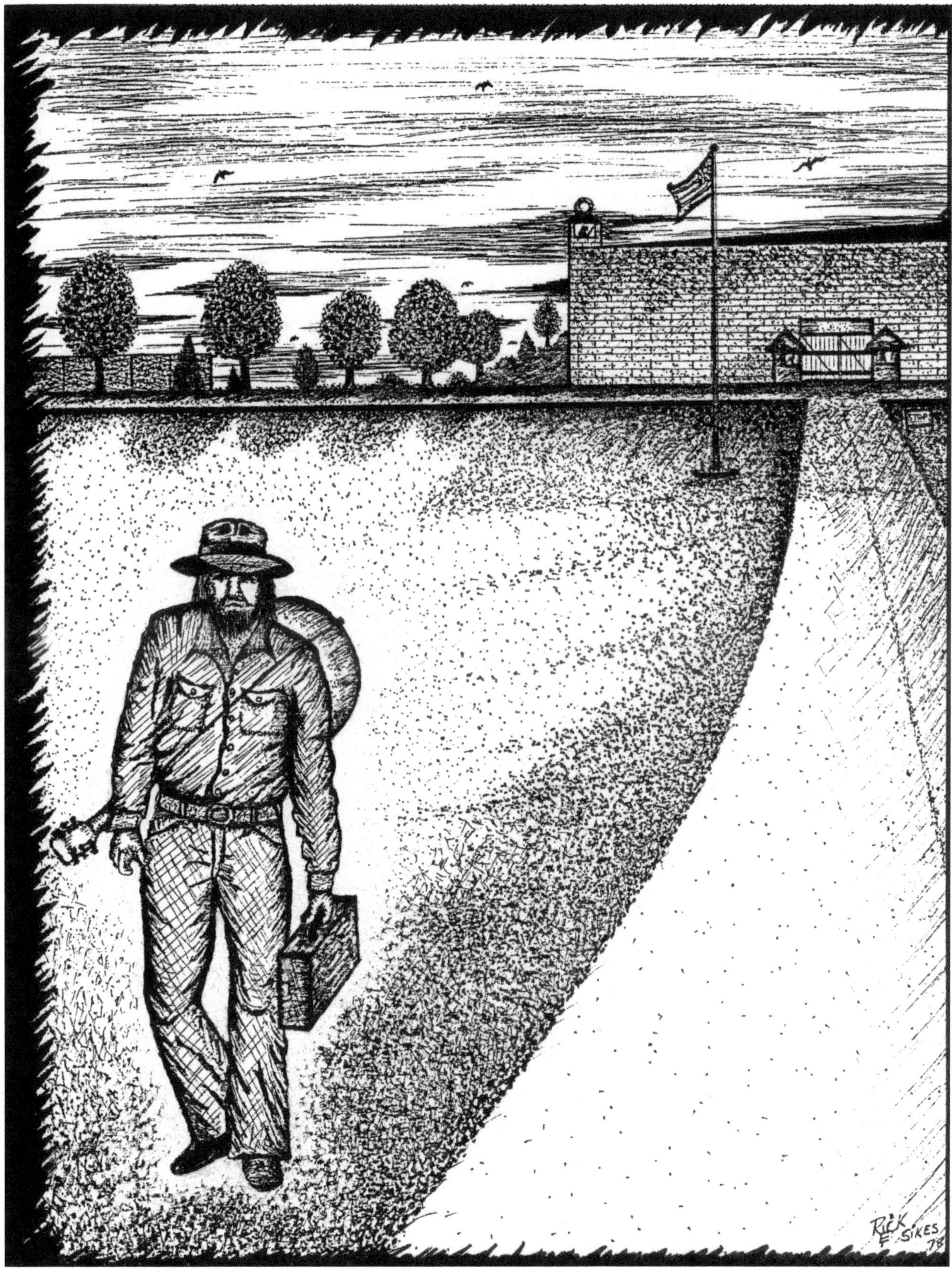

## *Convict's Homecoming*

Ann, you better than anyone, knew my goal

For a woman like you, men have cheated and stole

Thrown away family and friends, given their soul

Having tossed away their pride they have killed and they've died

You knew I didn't, yet you lied, the love I gave was all in vain

You betrayed me quickly, without any shame. There was more to it than you claim

What about the man you shielded from blame?

Knowing loneliness and pain you sacrificed me just the same

You knew when they took me away I would live in hell, a debt I didn't owe to pay

Twenty years in prison is a very long time to stay

Horrors I've been through, it's a wonder I'm still sane

You laughed in my dreams, played on my brain. Did you ever expect to see me again?

Ain't it surprising how swiftly the years fly?

When in a cell, time drags slowly by

No, don't explain, don't even try

Don't fear me, I won't harm you; wipe the tear from your eye

When they took me away to prison, did you cry?

You suffer more living - knowing...I hope you never die!

# *The Convict's Guitar*

Stories of times, places far away and near

Of bad times, good times, loneliness and love so dear

Where living is reality, not untouchable tomorrows afar

Stories from the soul, played on a convict's guitar...

Behind these high walls, lost and saddened hearts wail

Ballads mourning for life come from deep within the cells

Today lasted forever and well left its scar

Unnoticed, another tear falls on a convict's guitar...

Pitiful realization that yesterday and hopes are gone

A dead mind is buried in memories while the body lives on

Reality screams, "You are here! Does humanity know you are?"

No one hears the sad refrain of a convict's guitar...

Play upon those golden strings, my friend, a few of us still care

Even though the world has turned cold and unaware

Your song echoes truth from a bright and distant star

Melodies ring eternally from a convict's guitar...

## *Things Money Can't Buy*

The foolish things I did for money,

Trying to buy happiness for us, Honey.

You have tried to put it out of your mind,

That I will be gone a long, long time.

True, you have known a portion of hell.

I have had my share here in this cell.

Have courage, don't be afraid,

Someday I'll be home, when the debt is paid.

We will forget the sorrow and misery.

So things can be like they used to be.

This will be a story old.

One oft' times to be told.

Of a lesson learned so well,

Life is too short to sell.

Hurting and long lonely hours alone.

Too soon youth has flown.

Those tears we can't un-cry.

Things that money can't buy.

## *Love Effort*

Love is like a mountain

Sometimes it's steep

When you can't climb it

Then, sit there and wish and weep

Because, it's everything or nothing

Now, someday you may even want me

Others have before

Most of them slip my mind today

Yesterdays do fade away

Life is just that sort of thing

Lonely people sad songs do sing

I have sung a few of my own

But, when it's gone, it's gone

No need to stare at that peak

If the top of the mountain you seek

Make the effort, love is the effort

## *The Bandito*

Villain, hero, thief, and martyr of poem and song

Right in riches, in poverty wrong

Feared by the weak, cheered by the strong

Some who drank his wine, sat his table often

Deceitfully wished to see him in a coffin

For stately he stands as they could never be

Kind in heart, unselfishly free

Character noble, like the strong oak tree

Aware of self-failings, man among men

Standing faithfully to the end

Sharing with those he calls friend

Knowing his destiny from days of old

Life cannot be sustained by silver nor gold

Taking from abundance, in need giving

Self-sacrificing brings joy to living

Seldom reaching days of silver hair

Precious time with others does share

Hated and loved, the victim of strife

In honor, he will lay down his life

With the chase ended, his body in the ground

Curse him softly; the elusive rascal may yet be around

In rhyme and verse, I have explained it

But known only to himself is the heart of the Bandit

## *To A Friend's Best Dog - Man*

Well, here it is raining again,

Been lonesome since I don't know when.

Damned if I ain't always been!

Soft fingers of memory trace my mind.

Looking back on yesterday I find,

Long, long ago, way back then,

Before my old dog died, I had a friend.

Only a fool would go on.

My life has all been wrong.

I've been down much too long.

The curse is on me, I can't shake it.

Some fool says life is what you make it.

Sadly, I say with a sort of grin,

"Yes, before my old dog died, I had a friend."

Seems there is no good way to choose,

Everywhere I've been was bad news.

Hard luck walks in my shoes.

Calling me brother, a few came to my side,

Every time I trusted, I found they lied.

I did have one pal, true to the end,

Yep, before my old dog died, I had a friend.

## *Love And Peace*

Made up my mind tonight

To leave you and trouble behind

I searched my soul for a reason to stay

Not one could I find

You bring nothing but strife and grief

My life is missing love and peace

I want no more pouting, no more crying

I'm tired of you messing with my mind

When the sun comes up in the morning

It's all gonna cease

I'm liberating you, woman

So I can find some love and peace

Life ain't nowhere spent grieving

I've said it before many times in the past

This time, I'm really leaving

That ol' road will be relief

Nothing left to say, except you can kiss my ass

May we both find love and peace

## *Love Like Hell (For Lovin's Sake)*

Traveling to gigs in a beat-up car

Watching the sunsets, wishing on a star

Those ol' Texas roads were narrow and long

But, I had you, and we had a song

It was easy back then to give and take

And love like hell, for lovin's sake

In that poverty ridden playground yard

Times were tough, things were hard

We were poor, but rich back then

You could smile, I could grin

We dreamed of that monster hit I'd make

And loved like hell, for lovin's sake

Never a moment to call yours and mine

Since they say we've made the big-time

Guess it always happens this way

It's a hell of a price to pay

Let's just slip off, take a break

Then love like hell, for lovin's sake

## *Gone Again*

Woman, you ain't hearing a word I say!

See those leaves falling when the limbs sway?

Soon you'll see that summer was yesterday,

Like the wild geese, your man, gone astray.

When the ship of love started failing,

You didn't even know it stopped sailing.

For too long now, I've done all the bailing,

It's sink or swim, I'm throwing the towel in.

Who is gonna' care if you're crying?

Nobody wants to hear your lying.

I'm damned tired of trying!

What ain't dead, is bound for dying.

Maybe you will want me back then,

Ain't no use, I am gone again.

Just like it has always been,

Going, going, gone again!

## *The Troubadour's Woman*

When I was weary and the road was long

You gave me a song

When I felt I'd traveled my last bone-tired mile

You gave me a smile

When there seems no tunes are left on my old guitar

And I need a melody, there you are

I sing of sorrow and hard times

But, find you ever easy on my mind

I do all I can think to do

You give me ideas fresh and new

I grow restless and unsure

Your understanding makes me secure

They say a man's song is his soul

You are the story I have told

"Let us have a good day today, for we are making memories for the future, with each passing moment."

## *Sometimes A Friend*

You wonder where I'll be when the night is gone

If dawn will find me far away, you alone

Your lips and arms are welcome and warm

I mean to never do you no harm

Maybe I'll pass this way again

Sometimes a man needs a friend

Loving is different with a traveling man

Don't try to know me, don't try to understand

You couldn't see what motivates me

It's inside, so let it be

Tomorrow is a new song in the wind

Another time, another friend

Don't get love looks in your eyes

This is the moment you must realize

What I say is for your sake

When I go, memories are all I take

Remembering how tonight has been

A man sometimes needs a friend

# "STEAM TRAIN" MAURY GRAHAM - THE HOBO KING

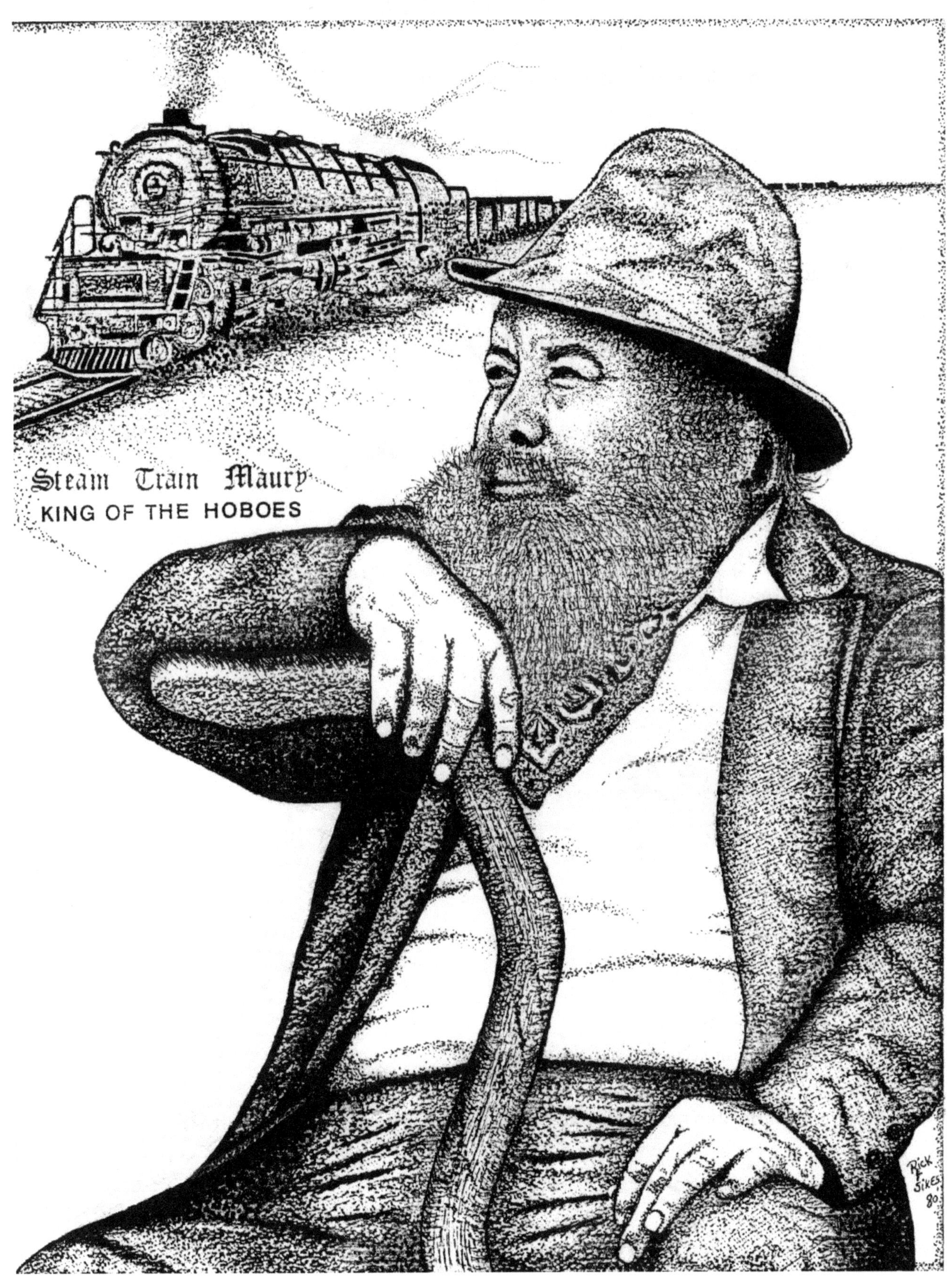

## *The Hobo King*

In Loving Tribute to Steam Train Maury Graham, The Hobo King

For the vanishing hoboes and the Hobo King

Freedom's merry jingle let us sing

Ruts of roads he's traveled are lines above his brow

Freedom of the past, are the stories he tells now

Hair and beard white as snow

Dancing eyes blue as the Ohio

Smiling like early morning sunshine

Ol' Steam Train still rides the line

Long live the hoboes and the Hobo King

They rode the Burlington Northern, Union Pacific, Rock Island and Santa Fe

Chicago Northwestern, L&N and South Seaboard along the way

Some were looking for jobs or a home

Others just had wanderlust to roam

Open skies, campfires, smoke of coal

And powerful locomotives bound their soul

They rode 'em and showed 'em for all to see

Freedom is for those who have the courage to be

Long live the hoboes and the Hobo King

*THE NEXT COMPILATIONS ARE FROM THE PEN OF JAN SIKES*

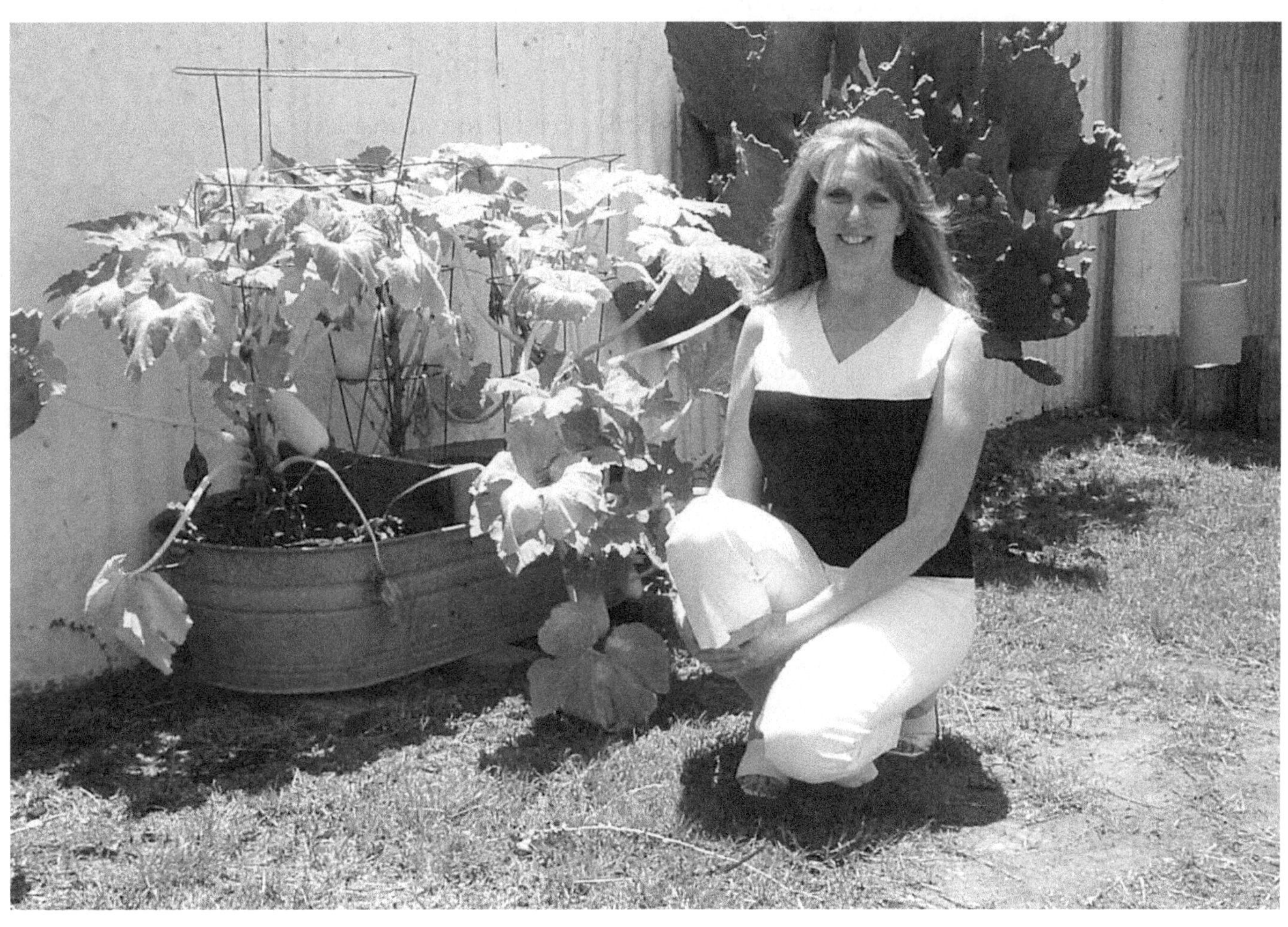

## *Comes the Dawn*

After a while you learn the subtle difference
Between holding a hand and chaining a soul
You learn that love doesn't mean leaning
And company doesn't mean security
Eventually, you understand that kisses aren't contracts
And presents aren't promises
Then you start to accept your defeats
Head up and eyes open wide
With the grace of a woman, not the grief of a child
And learn to build your roads on today
Because tomorrow's ground is too uncertain for plans
Futures have a way of falling down in mid-flight
After a while you learn that even sunshine
Burns you if you get too much
So you plant your own garden and decorate your own soul
Instead of waiting for someone to bring you flowers
And you learn that you can endure
That you really are strong
You truly do have worth
And you learn and learn
With each goodbye - you learn

## *My Pledge*

Today I stand here next to you

To pledge my love – faithful and true

At your side I'll always be

From now throughout eternity

And so, in the sight of God and man

I promise as I take your hand

To love you deep and strong and true

And with you be, though storms may brew

Never may our love get cold

Even though we'll both grow old

So, today they will say I belong to you

Although that fact <u>we</u> already knew

**This poem was written as part of Jan and Rick's wedding vows**

## My Pending Joy

Why must I allow it to be?

This deeply rooted ecstasy

To yet still remain in hiding

While all along I should not be denying

My love, my love, when will I see

That my pending joy is not fantasy?

For years now, it's been always pending

While day by day, I live only existing

Isn't it time that my joy becomes reality

Instead of an elusive tomorrow that never I see?

A rare and wonderful love you are giving

That comes not often to we creatures who are living

My joy must surely now pending cease to be

And be my daily strength as I wait for you to be free

## *Leavenworth and You*

Checked into a motel in Leavenworth, Kansas
Drove all that way; had to have some answers
You see there was this man I had loved for a long, long time
He'd written me long letters; said he wanted to be mine
I brought my daughter with me to the penitentiary that day
We surveyed the walls and gray structure with nothing to say
Our reunion inside was a true celebration
Really it was worthy of publication
And that is why I take pen now
To relate to you our solemn vow
There we sat on that $28^{th}$ day of June
In the stark prison visiting room
We spoke of love and truth and freedom
Our dreams took shape as boldly we spoke them
We had woven a spell – long before you sat in that cell
So I guess you've figured out by now
Exactly what was that solemn vow
Yes, we swore to live as mates
A lifetime or more with no restraints
I felt at peace and so very content
To return home with full intent
To plan and work and prepare
For my man to come and take his chair
At the head of our table
For as long as he is able
And we will be
His family
To the ultimate degree

# *I Am You – You Are Me*

I don't know how it came to be

That we in spirit love were joined

Somewhere out in eternity

Then split apart like a germinating seed

And placed on earth each other to seek

We looked in many stranger's eyes

Only to turn away and recognize

That this was not the one we sought

You and me

Then at last, fate heard our plea

And now forevermore we'll be

Bound in love

By satin chains and golden threads

And endless love where we make our bed

And never again will we part

For we are joined heart-to-heart

From Spirit World to earthly plane

We'll never need to search again

In love with you, I am set free

For I am you and you are me

## *Liberty's Lament*

The orange sun dawns over the quiet plain
An innocent land – no traces remain
Of the blood that was shed or lives laid down
In a struggle for liberty from under the crown.
"Independence," they cried, "We must be free!"
And the flag waved high – "O say can you see"
Battles were fought; battles were won
Then progress began and soon there was none
Of the glow of victory or unity of cause
And freedom's perfection unveiled its flaws
The red sun set on a crowded avenue
A young girl weeps in anguish, her dreams rent in two
A small baby whimpers, huddled close to her breast
No victory for these – only plaintive protest
Does no one see? Does no one hear?
The reasons for the battles are no longer clear
Huddled in the shadow of the Statue of Liberty
"Independence," she sighs, "Oh where can it be?"
Something got lost along the way
Perhaps we'll gain it back all back someday

## *For My Husband*

I don't know how to say this well

I love you more than words can tell

To you, I give my heart and soul

With you only, am I made whole

You are my bright and shining star

Together we will travel far

On this journey of life we do embark

And promise true to never part

And so, my love, this is short and sweet

But the message is full and complete!

## *Homecoming*

You've been gone for way too long

It's been a sad and lonely song

Now the sun is peeking through

They've said, "Okay, you've paid your due."

They are letting you go

I can hardly believe it is so

Being apart is totally wrong

'Cause together we truly do belong

Now we'll finally have our chance

To know complete, love's true romance

The children are more than glad

They'll at last, have their Dad

And I'll have the man I've always wanted

I promise you, my dear, our love will go undaunted

We will celebrate your homecoming

With happy tears and lots of loving

Then we'll be wed

And forevermore I'll share your bed

You my husband, I your wife

This is the way we'll begin a new life

Welcome home, Darling!

## *Finding The Best Of My Dreams*

I once was a young girl watched over and loved

Didn't know life could ever be sad

I grew up believing God lived up above

And that fairy tale dreams could be had

I put them together one dream at a time

The things that I wanted to do

And the one I enjoyed creating the most

Was the image of us two

I lived out my first dream by loving you

Then you were taken away

It was then I learned what pain could do

And how to live day-by-day

I continued to live and discover my dreams

But none ever topped finding you

Now soon, I'll be lying in your arms again

And my dreams are starting anew

Finding the best of my dreams

For the rest of my life

Floating down rivers and streams

Happy to be your wife

Looking for each new tomorrow

Leaving all worry and strife

Finding the best of my dreams

For the rest of my life

## *Life With A Man - For Sharon*

Life with a man isn't always easy

He'll come home with mud on his feet

And his clothes will get greasy

He'll whimper and whine when he's feeling ill

But when you are sick, he'll want his supper still

Oh, he's not all bad

And really kind of nice to have around

Especially when you're blue and sad

And not a friend can be found

And you know that he loves you

He'll protect you from harm

In the circle of his arms

You'll feel safe and warm

So, always be true and try not to be blue

When he forgets your birthday or the size of your shoe

And remember he's just a grown-up little boy

And as the woman in his life, you can bring him great joy!

# *Lewis*

Lewis, you were a good friend to me

I am indebted to you through all eternity

I'll never forget the gifts you gave

And how it was only love you craved

I laughed out loud at all of your jokes

You were more sincere than most folks

If I could now roll back the hand of time

I'd make sure you felt for one day that you were mine

I harbor regrets

We lost many bets

But, now you're gone; that can't be reversed

And all of your wealth will be dispersed

Tomorrow I will see you one last time

I hope you can look inside this heart of mine

And see that my friendship was sincere and true

There will never be another person quite like you

Wherever you are I pray that you are at peace

For you are now what they call deceased

## *Love's Frontier*

Testily, we humans dare to explore

The wonderful vastness of love's frontier

It is too obvious in life to ignore

Yet is the beginning of many a tear

In ancient times, it was praised o'er and o'er

The gods even craved it; that is very clear

It tugs and pulls at our very core

The intensity makes us quake with fear

We've barely begun to step through the open door

Although it's been studied for many a year

Its colorful shape, fashion and form

Creates in us feelings that are most sincere

A mother, a child, a lover and more

These are just a few ways that it can appear

It can take us to unknown heights and allow us to soar

Then in the blink of an eye, totally disappear

The mystery of love's elusive splendor

Permeates the very atmosphere

Confessions are made that love is our mentor

And is the one thing we secretly revere

So as we move forward and let love restore

Our life and our luster in love's vast frontier

We are driven to clamor again for an endless encore

## *The Lay-Off*

There came to Atlas one day, the big lay-off

Everyone worried; they had loans to pay off

They told us 100 employees would go

But, they did not say who, or when we would know

Some of the employees are retiring

And others are simply conspiring

To keep their jobs

Regardless the odds

So, impatiently we wait

And wonder and speculate

About who are the most likely candidates

To soon be put out the gate

## *I've Got To Write And The Moon Is Full*

I've got to write! The urge has hit

"I Love you Bobby" screams out in blue paint on the side of a small tin building

Are the fish biting?

Yes, perhaps it is a curse to be born black or brown or poor

I do not know...I think we have control over our plight.

Social pressures rule us

My heart pounds with fear

"Oh no! Please do not look at me!"

The kittens from last summer are still here

They are bigger and fewer, Remember?

Still untamed, distrusting, smart

Beautiful blue cloudless sky, sailboat smoothly gliding by

Greenish blue water ripples, metal swings harmoniously creak

Children happily play, birds chirp, Azaleas fluorescently bloom

It is Spring

This was at one time OUR Kingdom to rule

What really happened? Who is the real fool?

## *Haunted*

Haunted by your cutting words that burn into my mind

Tortured by the things you said, remarks that were unkind

You intensely condemned for choices from days and years gone by

You took my deepest confidence and turned it into a lie

You tore apart my self-esteem and made me hate myself

You turned on me with viciousness like a lion upon an elf

I've tried hard to let it go - Forget or justify

But suddenly, like a whirlwind from out of empty space

Your words across my wounded heart and mind begin race

They leave me helpless and weak

Crying and unable to speak

Haunted...Haunted inside my mind

## *The World Can't Change The TRUTH*

Why is it so? Everything seems so wrong. In Africa, children are starving. Why, even in America...yes, our own country, children are being abused in every way possible. Each winter, hundreds of 'old folks' freeze to death inside their own homes. Our penitentiaries are full and running over and yet murderers walk the streets threatening our well-being. Where did it start? How did it happen? The TRUTH existed when human-kind took the wrong turn. How is it, that this was allowed to be?

Perhaps, there was no wrong turn, or error made...

Even as I write, TRUTH is my constant companion. I may choose not to recognize him or acknowledge his presence, but he exists just the same. It's the little things that prove this to me, like that twinge of conscience when I am less than honest; the small still whisper that alerts me to someone else's dishonesty; or the sense of totality when looking into a baby's eyes. Then there are the big things that prove his existence like efforts once made by our nation's top entertainers called "USA Africa" that literally fed thousands of starving children in Africa.

"What about our own backyard?" you ask.

We are the determiners of our own destiny. We make the choices. They are not made for us. TRUTH exists within each human being alive. Yes, TRUTH can change the world, but it won't. We look for change through some mystical or far-out means when it can only happen through each of us taking the initiative to be responsible for our own destiny. We MUST make the choice to acknowledge TRUTH'S existence and act accordingly.

Yes, TRUTH can change the world, but only through each of us and only through conscious choice!

## *Surrender*

There is no shame in surrender when it is time

Like General Lee, you've known when to lay low and when to climb

I've watched you suffer for so many years

Your life seemed destined to one of pain and of tears

Yet you fought on – the valiant soldier in fierce battle

You boldly sang your song – rode tall in the saddle

You've now come down to the last battle call

You'll hang up your sword, tired and weary you will fall

But know that you've left many good marks behind

While you learned how to love and how to be kind

Taught lessons to all who shared your many paths

That will long be remembered after you've passed

There is no shame in surrender when it is time...

*About the Authors*

## RICK AND JAN SIKES

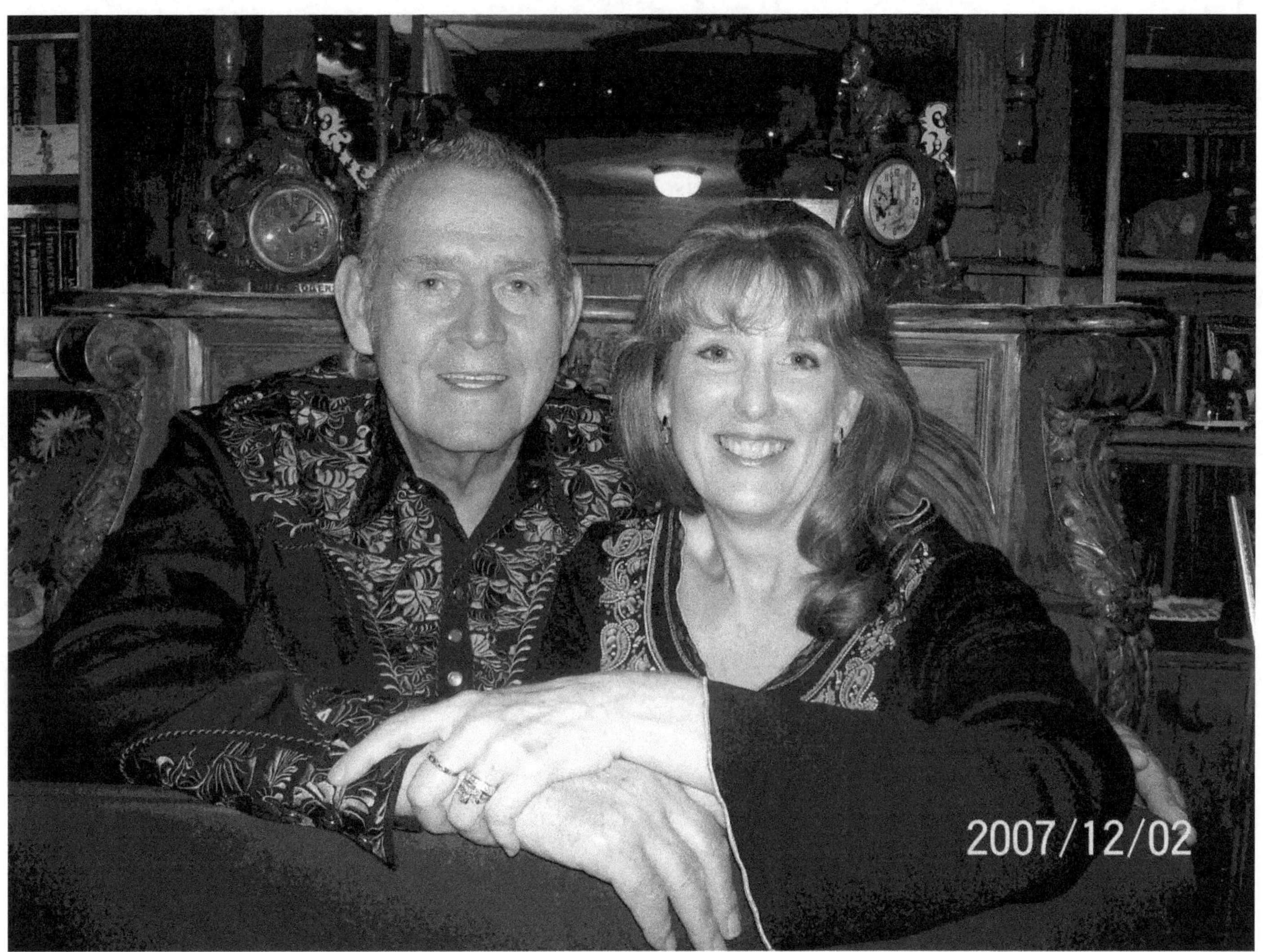

## RICK SIKES

James Richard (Rick) Sikes was born smack in the middle of the great depression. His family, although dirt-poor, were a proud people. At a young age, his father taught him to fire a rifle. He hunted meat for the family by the time he was twelve, along with his faithful collie, Fireball. How he loved the country and roaming through the hills and valleys of central west Texas. He discovered music, or maybe music discovered him at the age of fourteen. By the time he entered his senior year in high school, he had formed a weekend band, along with his childhood friend, Dean Beard. His music career took him down the roads of Texas, New Mexico, Oklahoma and out to California until, in 1971, he was arrested, found guilty and sentenced to seventy-five years in prison for two bank robberies.

Being convicted of a crime he had not committed, he arrived at the gates of Leavenworth Penitentiary, angry, bitter and rebellious. But, time has a way of smoothing out the rough edges of a man's soul. He spent every spare minute doing something creative with his hands and mind. He discovered who he really was and saw how he'd gotten lost along the journey down so many roads.

In this poetry and art book, you will find a sampling of the creative genius who lived inside Rick Sikes. You'll see his distorted sense of humor, feel the loneliness that permeated his being and get a glimpse of the world around him through his eyes. These poems are literal breaths of life from within a prison cell.

In 2013, Rick Sikes was listed in the *Texas State Historical Association Handbook* as a pioneer in Texas Music. In 2004, he was inducted into the Central West Texas Music Hall of Fame under the Rockabilly category.

Rick finished his earth journey on May1, 2009. His widow, Jan Sikes, has written his entire story through a series of four books.

If you enjoy these poems and art, please take a closer look at the books depicting his life.
http://www.ricksikes.com
http://www.jansikes.com

## JAN SIKES

Multi-Award winning author, Jan Sikes, began her writing journey around the age of eight.

But, it was after the death of her beloved husband, Rick Sikes, that she started the journey of telling their story. She believes with all her heart, there is something in them worth sharing. Bits and pieces of wisdom, hard-learned lessons and above and beyond all, love...True love that you read about in fiction stories...and yet this is truth. The old saying, *truth is stranger than fiction* fits these stories.

*Flowers and Stone* is the first book in this series. It is a passionate love story with a twist, set in the rowdy raucous honkytonks of Texas in 1970.

*The Convict and the Rose* continues the story and is set behind the walls of Leavenworth Penitentiary. It tells a tale about learning to think and do positive in a negative situation that inspires hope for making a better life regardless of the circumstances.

*Home At Last* is the third segment of the series and is set in Central West Texas. It is a story of starting over, struggles, triumphs and most of all of a love that never falters.

*'Til Death Do Us Part* ends the series. With sand in the hourglass growing thin, Luke and Darlina Stone face trials that would destroy a lesser man and woman. Time slows down to a crawl, life is measured in breaths and each breath comes with a price.

Jan also releases a music CD of original songs with each book that fits the time period of the story. Why? Because the stories revolve and evolve around a deep-rooted passion for music

She currently resides in North Texas, has five grandchildren and in her spare time, loves to volunteer at Texas music festivals. She serves on the Board of Directors for the Texas Musicians Museum, The Texas Authors Institute of History and The North Texas Book Festival.

www.ingramcontent.com/pod-product-compliance
Lightning Source LLC
LaVergne TN
LVHW081403110826
845149LV00010B/1650
* 9 7 8 0 9 9 0 6 1 7 9 6 9 *